THERE ARE
NO GOODBYES

THERE ARE
NO GOODBYES

GUIDANCE AND COMFORT FROM
THOSE WHO HAVE PASSED

ELIZABETH ROBINSON

HAY HOUSE, INC.
Carlsbad, California • New York City
London • Sydney • Johannesburg
Vancouver • New Delhi

Published and distributed in the United States by: Hay House, Inc.: www.hayhouse.com
Published and distributed in Australia by: Hay House Australia Pty. Ltd.: www.hayhouse.com.au
Published and distributed in the United Kingdom by: Hay House UK, Ltd.: www.hayhouse.co.uk
Published and distributed in South Africa by: Hay House SA (Pty), Ltd.: www.hayhouse.co.za
Distributed in Canada by: Raincoast Books: www.raincoast.com
Published in India by: Hay House Publishers India: www.hayhouse.co.in

Design by Rhett Nacson
Typeset by Bookhouse, Sydney
Edited by Margie Tubbs

ISBN: 978-1-4019-5079-8
Digital ISBN: 978-1-4019-3387-6

10 9 8 7 6 5 4 3 2 1

1st edition, September 2017
Printed in the United States of America

MAY THE WORDS ON THESE PAGES INSPIRE
THE AWAKENING OF CONSCIOUSNESS AND
HERALD A NEW VISION FOR A MORE
PEACEFUL AND LOVING WORLD

CONTENTS

THE CALL
THAT CHANGED
EVERYTHING

It was a cold January Sunday. The snow had melted but the sky was still overcast, forming a thick grey ceiling over our small southern Oregon town. After a busy week consulting, I was enjoying a quiet Friday evening relaxing on the sofa when, without warning, I felt a sudden and deep sense that someone I knew was in danger—not just in danger but in danger of losing their life.

This wasn't the first time I'd received a strong intuitive 'knowing' about something left of field. At first I wasn't sure of what to make of these random insights, but eventually I learnt to pay attention.

In a panic and searching for answers to this terrible feeling of despair, I was desperate to know who was it I had to try to protect. Something had to be done, though I had no idea what. I started by asking my daughter Jessica if her school friends were okay. 'Yes Mum,' she answered annoyed, 'everyone's fine. I am trying to watch the movie!'

Quiet now, I was still restless, unable to shake the feeling that something bad was about to happen. Finally I went to bed. Sleep came hours later.

After a very late night, I awoke late morning to a thick fog-like sensation, feeling overwhelmed, vulnerable and powerless. Then those intense emotions suddenly dissipated and all that remained was a sense of calm, of surrender.

After a late Sunday lunch, the phone rang. Answering it changed everything. 'Elizabeth, it's Elise here,' my friend began. Her tone was serious, as if there was something she was loath to share. 'I have some sad news about something that happened yesterday.'

Without thinking, I sat down on the third step of the staircase, just inside my front door. 'Are you okay?' I asked frantically.

Elise's gentle, loving voice came back on the line: 'Elizabeth, Shylo killed herself around lunchtime yesterday.'

For a moment I was unable to comprehend what Elise had said. I'd had my last consultation with Shylo only ... what ... four days before and she was fine, excited about continuing her work with me. I'd even had an email from her two days later, and she was really looking forward to our next session.

'It was Shylo's mother who passed on the news,' Elise continued. Shattered, my mind flashed back to my last interaction with Shylo, to her blonde hair tied neatly back in a ponytail, her thirst to know why her car accident had happened two years before. After our session, Shylo had driven me home. It had all been so normal and the conversation so positive. She'd spoken about her special diet and that she was going to buy some healthy food to eat before heading home.

I remembered telling her to take care and drive home safely, looking into her beautiful soulful brown eyes.

'I will,' she'd responded. 'See you next week.'

As she pulled away from the curb, little did I realise I'd never see her alive again.

I became aware of Elise's voice saying something about Shylo's mother.

'Oh God, it's so hard to make sense of this ...' I said in return. 'I didn't see it coming. I've worked clinically with suicide for years. There was no sign, no sign at all.'

'Her mum said the same thing,' said Elise compassionately, as my world shattered around me.

'What did she do? How did it happen?'

'All we know is she found her mother's gun and shot herself.' Elise's voice soft and gentle, trying to soften my response to the news she was sharing.

'Oh my God, a gun!' I replied, horror filling my every cell. 'There is something really strange about this though,' I continued through my tears. 'I can't explain it, but I just know there's some higher reason for this. I'm going to find out what it is. She'll have to come and explain this to me, explain to me why she made the choice she did.'

At that moment, a trapdoor seemed to open, plummeting me down into a dark place of guilt and personal accountability. Making my way into my bedroom, I stopped inside the door, sobbing uncontrollably.

'Why did you do it, Shylo?' I cried. 'Why didn't you call me? Why didn't you ask for help? I could have helped you through this ... I'm so angry with you that you did this! You had better come and tell me what the bloody hell this is all about!'

Sliding down the wall I slumped to the floor, my head buried in my hands. I had never lost a client to suicide. The thought of it was incomprehensible. That's why I had entered the counselling profession. Counsellors support people to feel better, to build resilience, to realise their greatness. Each person's life was precious to me. I treasured helping people through their challenging times.

Shylo had struggled so hard for two years to fight her way back from her accident. During our sessions, I referred to her as a 'warrior woman'— able to take on anything that life presented. A confident horse rider and A-grade student, Shylo was also hungry to understand her higher spiritual purpose. Her story had touched me. So too did her light and potential, they were so beautiful.

At her very last consultation I'd said: 'Shylo with all you have been through and all that you are, as you open up to life's deep wisdom at such a young age and walk forward into your future, you have the power to touch so many lives!'

My daughter cautiously entered my bedroom. 'What's wrong? What's happened?' she'd softly inquired.

'It's Shylo,' I spluttered, then told her the worst.

'It's not your fault Mum,' Jessica said, trying to offer support and comfort.

But that was little solace, as I was convinced I could have done something. I could have made Shylo feel differently, and now it was too late.

Sometime later, I called my dear friend and mentor, Dr John Mack, author, visionary and Professor of Psychiatry at Harvard Medical School. He was a beloved father figure to me. He was caring as usual, as he listened with great understanding to my confusion and despair. He reminded me of his early research on teenage suicide, highlighting that the majority of teen suicide is spur of the moment. After a brief conversation, we said our fond goodbyes.

Feeling emotionally exhausted and drained, I took solace in a long relaxing shower, grateful for the nurturing stream of warm water as it gently caressed my entire body. Closing my eyes, the water and its warmth flowed down over my hair and shoulders relaxing me. Then suddenly, I detached from my body. One part of me was aware of my body and the comforting stream of warm water, while another part of me rose up from my body, bathroom and home.

As I journeyed higher and higher, I wondered where I was being drawn to. Remarkably, I continued to rise through the layers of an ever-changing environment. The heavier confines of my grieving body rapidly became a distant memory as I rose up beyond the wider urban landscape. I drifted higher still into the expansive radiant energy of rivers, oceans and mountains, then higher again into even lighter luminous layers, where breathtakingly vivid colours invoked splendour, serenity and infinite conscious awareness.

Finally, I slowly rose through a cloud of bright white mist into an open space the size of a large room. As I looked up, I saw Shylo appear through a doorway. She was now luminescent and calm, full of warmth and light. As she walked effortlessly down several stairs and across the space towards me, there was a look of such radiance on her face. I was overwhelmed with joy, as love and gratitude engulfed my senses.

Immediately following, an intense feeling of tragedy and uncontrolled pain flooded my being. Desperately seeking answers, I gently asked: 'Why did you do it?' But the moment I spoke, I found myself slipping back down through the cloud-like layer of this sacred meeting space, away from Shylo. 'No, I'm not ready to go back yet!' I cried.

Shylo stood up, turned and walked back up the steps towards the door, unaffected by my response or my sudden retreat. As she climbed to the top step, she suddenly turned back towards me. Then with a wry look on her face, her eyes vibrant, she reached down a few inches away from her stomach and tugged on a thin cord that flowed from her body, stretching across the space between us.

At that moment, I felt a powerful tug at the centre of my belly, just below my navel. My consciousness immediately plummeted back to the shower, as my right hand slapped against my belly in shock. Peering down at my body I noticed a thin, gold cord connecting into my energy field. Amazingly, this cord somehow connected me to Shylo.

I stood mesmerised, frozen in a haze of shock and wonderment. Nothing could have prepared me for this.

What did it all mean?

The following day was my birthday. Sadness blanketed my heart. At various times during the day, I had a sudden awareness of what Shylo was experiencing in her place beyond the veil. It was almost like I could be there and in my own moment at the same time.

At one point, I could see Shylo walking along beside a very caring older woman, whose light brown hair was swept up loosely in a twist at the back of her head. As she walked with Shylo, the older woman listened compassionately, without judgement, holding space in a way that enabled Shylo to evolve beyond the choices she had made. They were walking along a beach, waves lapping over their bare feet. This wasn't a literal experience now, more like the re-experiencing of a fond memory they had shared while on earth. Somehow they were both able to connect with that memory, tangibly enough to recreate the experience in that moment.

I was so grateful for these glimpses into Shylo's new world, to share her unfolding moments, her adjustment to her new life.

Just after midnight, I climbed into bed but was unable to sleep. My room was now steeped in moonlight and my thoughts were with Shylo. Suddenly, I felt a distinct shift in the energy of the room. I was no longer alone. I sat up and looked over to the left side of the bed, feeling a slight chill. There in the shadows I immediately sensed, then saw, Shylo standing by my bed. 'I can see everything now,' she said in a soft, thoughtful voice. 'I didn't mean to hurt anyone. Can you tell them? Can you tell them?'

'Yes,' I whispered in reply.

'Can you tell them to put the things back in my room? I want the things left like they were. Tell Mum I like the things she's chosen for my funeral.'

Over the years, I've been able to contact those 'in spirit.' To begin with, they would often talk of something simple and personal, something very specific I had no prior knowledge of, so family members or friends knew beyond any doubt they were communicating with their loved one and that they lived on. Shylo's message was exactly that: evidence that her essential self, her soul, had survived the death of her body. I gently assured her I would pass on the message. Then from a place within me still desperate to understand why she had chosen to end her life I asked: 'Why did you do it, Shylo?'

Shylo quietly replied, 'I didn't want to think about it anymore,' before moving away.

I was apprehensive now she was leaving. There was an older woman near her, supporting her in these early stages of her transition and her reconnection with me. Could she be that same women I saw walking with Shylo along the beach? This older woman moved forward and tenderly explained: 'She needs to rest. She's been through a lot. She will only answer the questions she can for now.' Within moments, the woman was gone.

Had Shylo gone too? I waited, hardly breathing, my eyes searching the darkness. Shylo moved forward out of the shadows. 'Now I see there are always choices,' she continued. 'I could have just turned around to Mum and said: "Let's go out, let's just go out and talk about things." But I didn't. But maybe now I'm here, I can reach out to others who feel this way and help them see there are choices.' She paused, then added, 'They've asked me to assist you with your work to help others. I want to do that.'

At that moment, I sensed the power of her new awareness. Tears slid down my cheeks. Shylo had gained so much wisdom, but at incredible cost.

Two days later, I summoned the courage to phone Shylo's mother Jeanie, to give her Shylo's message. 'I have no idea what she means about putting the things back in her room and keeping it the way it was, but I hope it makes sense and brings some level of understanding,' I explained anxiously.

Jeanie began to cry, yet there was joy in her voice: 'We needed some photos of Shylo to use at her funeral. So we went into her bedroom and took some of her photos off the wall. I actually spoke out loud to her as I did it. I told her I'd put them all back after the funeral. I felt her there with us ... I felt a little nervous about it really. I knew she would not like us changing her room. She'd just had her room changed around only a short while back and, after that, she was always so fussy about her things being touched or moved by anybody else.' Jeanie continued with joy and grief in her voice: 'This is why I know it was her. I definitely know she spoke to you. This is just so typical of Shylo and it's something you just couldn't have known about. Okay Shylo, they'll go back on your wall,' she promised. 'I'm so happy she's alright. Being able to communicate with you from where she is now must be a great comfort to her ... I love her, and I miss her so much,' Jeanie added, breaking into tears.

That first communication from Shylo marked the beginning of a very special friendship. It was the beginning of the most challenging, powerful, yet transformational year of my life.

GLIMPSING DEAD PEOPLE

My extraordinary journey with Shylo changed the way I saw so many things. Yet when I look back, I can see how it also helped make sense of a series of unusual experiences I'd had as a child. Like many, I'd learnt early I was different from others—different from my family too, which isn't an easy experience to deal with, as we all long for acceptance and belonging. Yet as Shylo's visitations became more constant in my life, I began to realise that being a bridge between worlds was a role I had been playing all my life.

I was a creative and sensitive child, who loved to escape into my piano playing and ballet dancing, as they helped me deal with the disharmony and chaos that's often a part of family life. It wasn't just my emotional sensitivity that left me feeling different. I'd been able to sense those in spirit from quite a young age. While playing, I'd often feel the presence of someone watching me, and would suddenly stop and feel overwhelmed by a creepy familiar knowing. Someone else was there. Someone I didn't know. Yet when I slowly turned my head and dared to look, everything was normal. The eleven-foot ceilings, the antique Victorian grandmother and grandfather chairs with their quaint tapestry footstools and the tall antique vase on the mantelpiece proudly displaying my mother's flower arrangement from our garden were all in their usual perfect places.

Yet I knew there was more.

This ability to move between worlds can be really hard for children, as they rarely talk about such things or know how to deal with them. So they're left trying to navigate their unusual gifts alone. It was those moments, when I found myself alone in the family home or later at night when activity slowed and my sensitivities increased, that I found the most challenging. I often felt scared of being on my own in the dark, with the distinct feeling some unseen presence was watching me.

One particular night, I suddenly opened my eyes to see and hear all the objects in my room shuddering and shaking. As it turned out, my town was being hit by a violent earth tremor. More disturbingly, as I looked around my room I discovered people dressed in early settler clothing, standing at the foot of my bed. As they stared at me, they knew I could see them too. I could feel it, sense it. They knew there was something different about me. This was the most unnerving thing of all.

There were some places where I played that felt more intense. The spare land behind our family home was always a source of childhood fascination and fear. Whether I was playing with friends on the old cartwheel in the middle of the empty land, or sitting alone on my back gate that led into this area, I would sense an eerie foreboding as I looked across to the back of the house from there. My legs always pedalled faster when riding my bike past a particular old home on the hill.

Years later, I discovered that this home was designed by local architect Edmund Cooper Manfred as his grand Victorian mansion. It was built on the infamous 'Gallows Hill,' once used as a flogging post and gallows. A particularly significant public hanging took place in November 1831. Two convict servant men were hanged for the murder of a local man. Suspended in a gibbet and chained in iron hanging cages, they were left to die.

Another grand Victorian house with high ornate ceilings and large formal rooms, just several houses from mine, was the home of my best friend Sally. One day when she and I were alone playing together upstairs in Sally's bedroom, we both began to sense something in the room that we couldn't explain. There was a distinct feeling that someone else had entered the room. Standing still, we looked around nervously. We were no longer alone. In the very next moment, the blinds on the windows began to tremble. It was enough to make Sally and I run downstairs to the safety of the ground floor.

When I reached the bottom of the stairs, I looked back up to the landing. Standing there was an elegant woman, her hair tied back neatly in a high soft bun. She was wearing a long skirt and long-sleeved, high-collared white shirt, her hands gently clasped one over the other. I stared at her, struggling to comprehend what I was seeing and the terror it created.

Sally and I took refuge under the table tennis table in the large playroom at the very back of the house. Within moments, we heard the piano playing. Sally yelled out to her older sister Jane, who she presumed had returned home and was now playing the piano, but got no response. Back we ran to the front section of the house, past the staircase and into the dining room where the piano was located.

Everything seemed so still, as if the very objects were watching us. The music had stopped. But our relief turned to terror when we realised Jane was not playing the piano. No-one was playing the piano. We were all alone in that grand old house.

Screaming, we ran as fast as we could into the corridor, past the grand staircase and small kitchen, and back out to the playroom. Once again we took refuge under the large table tennis table, until moments later Sally's mother and several of her siblings walked through the back door, laden with groceries. Sitting perched on the high brown kitchen stools, we shared our story with Mrs. Dixon, who was unable to give us any explanation as to what had really occurred.

It didn't seem to matter whether I was visiting other local houses or was in my own family home. Any moment could suddenly become a confronting one. Entering the front section of our old late Victorian home

THERE ARE NO GOODBYES

at night took a great deal of courage. I'd slowly make my way towards the dark hallway, aware of a foreboding presence there.

Later, my older sister told me of her nervousness entering the front hallway at night. More recently, my mother shared her own disturbing experiences of that very same hallway as a teenager. On several occasions, she clearly heard piercing screams from what sounded like a terrified woman. Her mother also had similar experiences, but no-one had any explanation.

My grandmother was clairvoyant, and would often give tarot readings for friends seeking guidance. She would also read teacups. Eventually my mother threw her tarot card deck in the fire, believing the cards had something 'evil' about them.

Throughout my childhood, my mother would regularly talk about her prophetic dreams, her strong gut feelings, and other strange experiences that fascinated me. Yet when I shared my own unusual experiences, my mother would dismiss them as imagination.

Many years later, I came to understand that this was her attempt to allay my fears. If what I saw wasn't real, then I would have nothing to feel afraid of. Mum would regularly quip: 'It's not the dead you need to be afraid of, it's the living!'

MY COUNSELLING
CAREER BEGINS

Leaving my parents and small hometown at eighteen, I moved to the city to attend university. After I finished my counselling degree, I became a clinical medical social worker in a large teaching hospital. At any given time, I could be involved in an attempted murder or industrial accident, an attempted suicide, a shooting or car crash, or a political trauma and torture case. The job was intense and high stress. The two-hour commute usually gave me time to de-stress.

During my first few months, I came to know the Director of the Haematology Department. Almost every morning we'd walk past each other, meeting up somewhere around the operating theatres. There'd always be the same warm smile, a light 'good morning' or 'hello.' Soon this forty-something, tall slim strawberry blonde-haired man became part of my work life at the hospital.

Early one evening, about six months after I began working at the hospital, my colleague Rebecca and I left our office and walked along the glass walkway past the theatres to sign off for the day. Chatting lightheartedly, we rounded the corner from the operating theatres to the old section of the hospital, and saw the Director of Haematology making his way slowly towards us.

As I continued to talk with Rebecca, I noticed he seemed strangely dishevelled and had a vacant stare. Though he was tall with pale skin, his skin seemed even lighter than usual, almost translucent in the fluorescent light of the corridor. As we passed, I felt suddenly drawn to look directly into his face and quietly offered him a friendly 'hello.' Rebecca also lifted her eyes to acknowledge him. He simply turned his head ever so slightly towards us, and in one fluid motion gazed at me. He seemed almost to stare through me. His demeanour was flat and unresponsive.

Rebecca and I continued down the corridor chatting, as our workday drew to a close. We signed off for the evening then walked to the nearby train station for the long journey home. Another uneventful Monday night had passed.

Late on Friday afternoon Rebecca and I were sitting in our office, when we had an unexpected visit from the Clinical Specialist Social Worker from the Communicable Diseases Unit. He told us how the Director of the Haematology Department had hanged himself the previous Saturday evening at his home. His wife had found his body.

Looking across at Rebecca I replied: 'No, that can't be right! Rebecca and I saw him about 5pm on Monday night in the corridor near the theatres. I know it was Monday night because I've been off sick since then.'

'But Monday was two days after he killed himself. How can that be?' said the Clinical Specialist Social Worker.

Now perplexed, I said: 'But you saw him too, didn't you Rebecca?'

'Yes,' she replied. 'I saw him in the corridor. I just looked up to see him briefly. Elizabeth spoke to him.'

Shocked and searching for an explanation, I wondered how we could have seen this man walking past us in the hospital two days after he had actually ended his life. As I kept coming back to this question, I began to sense this was another piece in the picture puzzle of life that invited me into its reality. Somehow I just couldn't let it go. It wasn't so much that I had witnessed something unusual or confronting. These extraordinary experiences showed up in my ordinary moments and broke the trance I had been living in, altering the very nature of my reality.

Since then I have met and worked with many people who have had unusual life-altering experiences. Overcoming the obstacles of feeling alone within their experience, feeling misunderstood and marginalised, they have each learnt how to use their 'unusual' experiences to galvanise their personal and spiritual growth. This is the gift of these experiences. They are life's invitation to better understand ourselves and see our world in a whole new light. They help teach us resilience, so we can better navigate a society that is still largely unaware and unconscious of deeper experiences.

My life, I realised, was rich and multi-layered. I'd survived the trials of feeling different as a child. My clinical career was burgeoning and romantic love was blossoming. I felt that the life and love I longed for was crystallising.

The day finally arrived to attend my university graduation ceremony. I hired a white stretch limousine to take us on a sunset tour of the city harbour, before our celebratory family dinner. Sitting in a restaurant high above the city, I raised my glass to toast my parents for supporting my higher education and qualifications. As we clinked our glasses, my eyes met those of my boyfriend Mark, who I'd met in the third year of my degree. Classically handsome with dark hair, strong masculine features, athletic and a little over six foot one, he was hard to resist.

Within weeks, we had become engaged and the following year we were married. Two years later, when I gave birth to our beautiful daughter Jessica, my life began to take a more profound turn.

4

TUNING IN

Mark and I lived in an old house only a block from a huge city park with grand old trees, a serene lake and abundant bird life. This beautiful haven became my sanctuary. We had enthusiastic plans to renovate then sell our home, but a special nursery for our beautiful baby daughter was our first priority.

But here too I would suddenly have the unnerving feeling of being watched, while washing the dishes or cooking. One day I shared my experience with my friendly Italian neighbour Maria, over the top of her trellised tomatoes. Maria suddenly became quiet, explaining that an Italian woman who lived in my house in the 1950s had tried to gas herself. Though Maria was unsure whether the lady had died from the incident, she never recalled seeing the woman from that point on.

As my sensitivity was heightening, I developed a great thirst to know more. After speaking with a friend, I decided to book a psychic reading with a woman she'd seen and recommended. This was the first time I had done anything like this and I was understandably nervous.

What was the psychic going to look like? Was she able to read my every thought? What insights was she going to reveal? Was she going to tell me something that I didn't want to hear?

I felt anxious as I drove into her street. However to my surprise, when she opened her front door a completely typical middle-aged woman greeted me. I was ushered inside. Everything appeared comfortingly normal. 'Mind if I smoke?' she asked, as she casually lit her cigarette. 'What's your date of birth?' she continued in a businesslike manner. Then, copious quantities of personal information were revealed. She spoke about the challenges in my life, my likes, dislikes, travel experiences and health.

This was confronting. How could she pick up on so much detail, without previously knowing anything about me? Staring at the numbers she was scribbling down furiously, she looked more like an accountant doing a tax audit. She informed me I would soon be healing people.

'Me, healing people? How?' I asked, bewildered.

'Oh, with your hands.' Her reply was casual, matter-of-fact. Then, with her eyes fixed on the page in front of her, she quickly drew again on her cigarette.

To her this information seemed normal and acceptable. To me it was weirdly confronting, yet strangely familiar. 'Oh, I can see that you will also be able to hear information from the spirit world in your mind; it's known as telepathic communication,' she continued. 'Your main path, your purpose in this lifetime, is a spiritual one,' she said, leaving my mind in a blur.

I was taken aback. Until now, my life had been fairly straightforward. I had supported my husband to begin a new business as a property developer. We were both enjoying regular dinners out, fashionable clothes, cars, life's little luxuries. We dreamt of making even more money, so we could buy an even larger house. Suddenly, I had been woken from a long, materially-based sleep into a whole new world, nothing like the one I envisioned. Somehow I possessed abilities that I would use to help others.

Within three days I called to book a second appointment. There was so much more I craved to know. It was as if all my life I had lived in a grey colourless world, then suddenly I had been introduced to colour.

A week later I was knocking on her front door. This time when she opened it, she was more reserved.

'Why have you come back then?' she asked.

'Well, I have so many more things I want to know, so many questions, so much direction and guidance I feel I need,' I replied.

'If you need more guidance, then you can just take yourself off down to my back room and get it for yourself. You are just as capable of doing this as I am!'

This lady revealed a knowing that took me to a deeper place within. It was a place that felt mysterious, infinite and strangely familiar. I was effectively launched into a frenzy of self-discovery and seeking of spiritual truth. I had to know more.

This was before the massive explosion of self-help books and psychic TV shows. There was no internet, emails or social media connectivity. So I began to simply pray for direction and guidance to help me find my way. My daughter Jessica was then just two years old. I was a full-time mother and housewife. I wanted to take full advantage of the special years with my most precious little girl. So I took the opportunity to use her afternoon sleep time for meditation and self-inquiry.

In these moments of quietness and contemplation I would be very patient and simply observe what unfolded, rather than feeling like I had to control anything. It was a state of openness and trust. Before long I'd begin to see a swirling shape of colour in my mind's eye, as I deepened my level of relaxation. I slipped fully into a peaceful state of letting go. Then my body would suddenly become filled with an intense energy that was wise, loving and pure. This powerful energy intensified as I continued my practice. It was as if the universe was responding to my yearning to know more, experience more. This new and fascinating world was more compelling than anything I had ever experienced before. It was not something away from me, but a part of me. I found my intuition grew, helping me see my choices and make good decisions. It guided me into a deeper expression of myself.

For the very first time, I felt my soul begin to awaken. My spiritual journey became my life's passion. I began to experience a feeling of love so powerful, so unconditional it often moved me to tears. I'd never felt such unconditional love. It pervaded every cell and left me with such a deep reverence for everything around me.

After each session, I would notice how much greener and more beautiful the trees looked. The blue of the sky was more striking than before. Something deep inside me began to recognise and remember this heightened state of awareness. This ability to experience life more fully, lovingly and intently was what I had been missing all my life.

One night, not long after I had begun my relaxation and meditation, I heard a woman's voice ask: 'Could you help me? I am lost, and I can't seem to find where I am?'

Though shocked, I replied instinctively: 'Look for the Light and go into it. Don't be afraid; there is only love waiting for you there.'

It seemed that my sojourn into the world of meditation and spiritual energy opened a connection to the spirit world. At first I found this challenging to accept, and would feel quite frightened by the whole experience. Like many of us, I was influenced by the terrifying depictions of psychic phenomena in movies and on television. But perhaps the voices were showing me there was life beyond the death of the physical body? So many questions began to take shape. What really happens when we die? Where do we go, and what's it like there? I also began to experience a strong clear knowing about things, to tune into information as if it were floating in the air around me.

One day, as I stood in the warm afternoon sunshine hanging out the washing, I suddenly experienced a random pouring in of information about a client of my husband's, who I knew nothing about. Within a short time, Mark arrived home. 'Oh, hi!' I said, eager to share the information I had just received. 'You know the big house you are building? His wife doesn't like the front door you've ordered, and she wants it changed.'

'Why, has she called? I spoke to her just twenty minutes ago. It should be all sorted by now,' my husband replied.

'No, I was just given a message about it.'

My husband remained silent. My attempts to try to explain my new-found psychic ability to him had been unfavourably received. Perhaps he wondered if I was going crazy, but it felt effortless and normal to me. 'Oh, and you had better phone your mother. She's really upset. Her dogs are very sick and she's had to take them to the vet,' I continued.

'Well, I find that very hard to believe!' my husband replied, then turned away and walked back inside.

I suggested he call her and see for himself. Strangely, I had no attachment to this information—whether it was correct or not. I felt only peace. It took Mark several days before he reluctantly phoned his mother, to discover she was very upset. Her champion show dogs had been at the vet all week. After the call, he put the phone down and walked away. His silence told me everything.

I was longing for support, interest and understanding. He saw the woman he had married changing into a woman he didn't understand and could no longer relate to.

It was at that point our paths began to separate. He began to involve himself even more in his business, working longer hours and increasing his workload. I began to seek out other spiritual friends who could support and honour my journey, and the new person I was discovering myself to be.

FALLING
THROUGH TIME

It was a typical summer day. Clear blue skies, parched earth, the slow whir of ceiling fans and relentless heat. Thankfully, we had taken a lease on a house with a swimming pool. Its cooling waters beckoned.

Deciding to take Jessica for a refreshing swim, I placed her in her float vest and ring for safety. Then after swimming several laps, I took her out of her float ring to encourage her to swim more independently. She swam with me down to the deep end with great enthusiasm.

As I reached the deep end of the pool I turned. Jessica's little face was bobbing up out of the water. She needed something to cling onto. Telling her I was so proud of her, I encouraged her to swim towards me. By now I was treading water. Whisperings of the uneasiness I always felt in deep water stirred ever so silently. Ignoring the unease, I reached my arms towards Jessica, pulled her closer and tenderly cuddled her, allowing her to feel safe and supported.

In an instant, the entire pool and its surroundings disappeared. Instead of being in the afternoon sunlight enjoying a swim in my backyard pool, I was struggling to keep my head above water in the middle of a vast dark ocean. About forty yards to my right, I could see a huge eighteenth century sailing ship sinking. The scene was overwhelming.

I experienced an overpowering urgency. I was not alone in that swirling sea—my young son was in my arms and I was desperately trying to save us both. The sailing ship that was to take us to my husband, already stationed in Africa, was disappearing before our eyes. Soon there was nothing but the ocean—the deep vast powerful ocean.

My young son had not wanted to leave England. Convincing him of the adventure awaiting us, I had assured him we were in safe hands during the long voyage. While he had been apprehensive, I had remained buoyant, with an open heart and strong faith, determined to embark upon this journey.

Exhausted by the relentless waves and cold water, my strength was slipping away, taking with it my will to survive. A wooden crate tied with rope bobbed before me. If I could just reach it, perhaps it could help us stay afloat? Other debris floated lifelessly by in the water. I struggled to hold my son's face out of the black sea as it swirled around us. Then I noticed his eyes were closed, his body lifeless. My strength was fading fast.

Suddenly, my hand hit the edge of the pool. In an instant, my awareness was transported back to the present. Terrified, I pushed Jessica straight up out of the pool and onto the paving at its edge. Then without using the stairs, I heaved myself up out of the pool to the safety of dry land, staring with shock into the water.

Still stuck between two realities, I tried to comprehend this frightening experience, but couldn't make any sense of it. I scooped Jessica up in my arms and held her close to my heart. *What on earth had just happened? Where had I been? What the hell was happening to me?*

It was as if I had fallen through time and found myself completely somewhere else. Every moment was so vivid. I had no awareness of the pool or Jessica. Dazed and confused, I took Jessica inside, finding solace in a warm shower.

It was days before I summoned the courage to enter the water again. When I did, I had flashbacks of the previous experience, and felt just as confused about what had happened. Had I been somehow taken into my past? If it was a past experience, why did it feel so immediate, so real, as if it was only just taking place? Or was it still happening somewhere else at the same time? Wasn't time linear? Yet again, everything I knew to be real was being challenged.

This was not just a memory of an experience, it was very real. It began as a lingering memory that was somehow still held somewhere deep within me. I suspected it had been triggered by my anxiety at having to support Jessica in deep water. There were so many unanswered questions: *What was the true nature of reality? What was the purpose of such experiences?*

Reflecting back, I began to see a pattern emerge. As a child, although a member of my local swimming club I was certainly not a confident swimmer. All my life I had been afraid of deep water. Even in boats, I felt a sense of panic if the sea was anything other than calm. On several occasions I hid underneath the seat, crying to be let off the boat.

How many other past programs were running in my life I wondered (or indeed running my life), limiting my life experience without me consciously knowing about it? As my thoughts ran deeper, my questioning grew louder, and otherworldly experiences continued unabated. Something had been unlocked within me, something beyond my control.

Not long after the experience in my backyard pool, I lay in bed one morning while Mark and Jessica were organising breakfast. Enjoying the momentary peace, I closed my eyes. Within seconds, I was fully awake and staring at some roughly-hewn wooden floorboards. Next, a central mast came into view. As I looked up, I realised that I was in a small boat on an expanse of water. I was staring at another small wooden boat pulling alongside, and the face of a fearsome man in full Viking helmet. As I stared into his eyes I remember thinking: *Oh my God! What the hell is this?*

That one thought catapulted me back to my bed, with no idea where I'd been or what was happening. This time perhaps it had been a dream? Or perhaps I needed it to be a dream, so that my life felt more normal? Or was this experience trying to tell me that my everyday life was in fact the dream, and what was being so dramatically revealed to me was the true reality?

All I knew was that my ordinary life was being punctuated by events beyond anything I knew or understood. This was not a subtle or even gentle experience of awakening. This was a tough spiritual boot camp, and there was only one way through it: I had to surrender and grow. I had to liberate my awareness beyond its limitations, beyond certain perceptions that restrained the fullness of my understanding. I had to move out of my comfort zone, let go of what I'd expected life to be, and courageously face the unknown.

OTHER LIVES, OTHER EXPERIENCES

Around the same time, some significant things were happening with Jessica. One day she came in from collecting the mail, studying the envelopes confidently as she walked back up the paved driveway. As I held the door open for her, she exclaimed: 'Oh goodie! A letter from South America!'

There was no letter from South America, but I was intrigued as we didn't know anyone in that part of the world. It wasn't until she was three and a half that she elaborated more fully about South America. 'Mummy, I used to smoke when I was a man in South America. Isn't that yucky?' she announced, then went on to explain that she didn't have a car when she lived in South America, so had to travel to work by bus. That was something she'd never done in her life to that point in time. When I asked what kind of food she ate, she replied: 'Funny, spicy, pizza things.' When I asked her what sort of work she did, she replied: 'I made things with my hands.'

Throwing in a misleading question, I asked her to describe to me some of the things she could see as she travelled along in her car. Annoyed, she said: 'I already told you we didn't have a car!' At that point, she became quite fed up with me and changed the subject.

Our children are teachers. They stretch our understanding. At unexpected moments like this, the challenge for many parents is to remain present, open and interested in what they are sharing. It's essential to hold a space for psychically gifted children in a way that is non-judgemental. A key essential is to learn to listen with an intention to more fully understand what our little ones are telling us, being willing to receive whatever they are sharing from a place of interest and flexibility. Don't compromise the trust your child has in you in such moments. Children are very vulnerable to our responses. So it's crucial for parents to preserve that safe, healthy relationship with your child by not shaming, judging or criticising them. To do that successfully we need to parent mindfully, to be self-aware. The most essential requirement of any parent is to remain committed to our own personal and spiritual evolution.

Life was certainly getting a whole lot more interesting, since I'd opened up to the possibility that it was far more nuanced than I'd imagined.

On another occasion, I had woken up from a vivid dream of being a young woman in charge of a group of girls in a private boarding school in Austria, around the 1940s. The school was on a hill, and the country was at war. In one part of the dream, I saw enemy planes flying low in formation towards the hill. With the girls huddled close we crouched low, trying to shield ourselves behind one of the beds. My arms were outstretched to protect the girls from the looming danger.

About two weeks after this dream which I hadn't shared with anyone, Jessica announced she used to live in a school in Austria, high on a hill surrounded by lovely green grass.

'Was I there with you?' I casually asked.

'Yes, but you weren't my mummy. You just helped look after me,' she replied.

I noticed how easily Jessica accommodated an expanded sense of reality, how she looked at her relationship with me through a different lens. There was no confusion or conflict about these different roles we had apparently experienced together—her matter-of-factness about it all was the most revealing part. To her, other lives just weren't a big deal. She went on to describe how there weren't any boys at the school and how she and the other girls would often ride their bikes down the hill. She explained that she wouldn't get to see her mummy or daddy very often because: 'The mummies and daddies didn't live at the school with us.'

The following day, Jessica and I walked into a local shopping mall to be met by a lively display of Austrian folk dancing. I'd never seen anything like that in any shopping mall. Somehow things just kept unfolding with such perfect timing, as if by way of some higher well-synchronised script.

One night after this, an angelic being came to me in a dream. I was gently escorted down a corridor of life memories. It felt mystical and deeply peaceful. Groups of people, old friends and acquaintances, were standing along the passage. Each group we passed was connected to an existing memory in my near or distant past. Floating by each memory I observed it, recognised it and continued on. Finally, we moved beyond the passageway and stopped at a small round table where the angel said: 'It's time for you to move on.'

Her words were to herald significant changes in my life. The landscape of my life would never be the same.

A LOST BROTHER MAKES CONTACT

To assist our household financially, I returned to my clinical work as a professional counsellor three days a week. With medical team meetings, client and family interviews, written assessments, advocacy and liaison work, as well as counselling and intervention, my daily schedule was always demanding. I wasn't able to simply turn off my heightened 'sight' though, which often proved to be tricky. Aware of how friends, colleagues and family might react, I tried to keep my experiences secret, while working in this conservative environment. However, trying to hide my abilities for three entire days a week became increasingly challenging.

Tentatively, I began to share my insights with several colleagues. Hearing of my abilities, others began to approach me in the corridors or at lunch, seeking guidance or simply depth of conversation. I began to realise that people thirsted to know more about the world within and around them.

A flash of insight or a random 'vision' would take me by surprise during any average working day, just as it did on the day I received a message for one of our secretaries. Tina was a friendly, middle-aged mum from the UK, who had sweet dimples when she smiled and a good sense of humour. We got on quite well. As I was in a locum position and was new to the department, I hadn't had time to get to know everyone's background. So when I walked past her one morning after our intake meeting, I was intrigued to experience one of my strange otherworldly moments.

A whole stream of unsolicited information suddenly flowed into my mind. Scrambling for a pen, I diligently took notes. It was all about Tina and her accountant brother, who rode a motorcycle in the north of England. I was told about her grandmother, who'd passed some years earlier, and the afternoon teas she made for Tina when her mother came to visit. The information took almost the entire page. I had no clue what it meant; whether it was accurate or I had made it up. One thing I did know—I had to pass what I'd received on to Tina, which was awkward given it was a professional situation. As much as I'd have liked to ignore it, I knew I had to share this information because it was important for Tina.

Taking a deep breath I approached her. I handed her what I had written and quietly said: 'I don't know why, but when I sat down at my desk just now, all this information seemed to come to me. I wrote it down. It's about you. So I thought I should pass it on. I hope that's okay?' With that I smiled as if everything was totally normal, turned and walked back past the grey metal filing cabinets to my office. I closed the door, sat down at my desk, opened my patient notes and began to structure my next family intervention plan.

I was just about to call my next patient's wife, when Tina knocked on my door and came in. She sat on the chair and dissolved into tears. I sat staring back at her, concerned that I had upset her. 'I've been trying to locate my brother for the last two years,' Tina explained. 'He was adopted not long after he was born, but by the time my mum had me, she was married. So she kept me. It was only a few months ago that I received a letter about him. I had been told he worked as an accountant in the north of England and that he had two children—a niece and nephew I never knew about. But I was also told my brother had been killed in a motorbike accident only a year ago. I was too late you see.'

I sat with her as she cried. Then, just like the information had poured through me and onto the page minutes before, a sudden feeling of lightness entered the room. Tina took her glasses off, gently wiped her eyes and said: 'But what I really wanted to say was how much what you wrote meant to me. It's all true. But how did you know? How did you know about my grandmother and brother? I never told anyone here about all this!'

At that point I paused, wondering what I could tell her. How could I explain something I didn't fully understand myself? 'It just seemed to come to me to give to you,' I said simply. 'I don't really understand; for some reason, things like this seem to be happening to me. I'm glad it helped.'

With that, Tina left the room and I returned to my work. A few hours later there was another knock on my door. The social worker who worked in the Spinal Injury Unit asked me to come into her office when I was free. I agreed and entered her office about an hour later. Leanne was Malaysian and had a very soft gentle nature. She'd heard about my abilities and we talked for a while on a spiritual level. Then she shared that there was a very special Buddhist family who would be interested to meet me. Two siblings were Buddhist monks and one of the women was a Buddhist nun. The following day Leanne let me know that the family were looking forward to meeting me at their house on the following Saturday afternoon.

Leanne met me at the door when I arrived at their home. She introduced me to the elderly mother who spoke very little English. Removing our shoes, we walked into the main living room with its wooden parquet floor and whirring fans. The room was sparsely furnished. The entire family was seated on small flat cushions, on the left-hand side of the room under the windows. Feeling decidedly conspicuous, I experienced a sudden pang of nerves as they stared silently at me. One of them pointed to her forehead and said something. Leanne looked at me and smiled, then explained they saw a similarity between my high forehead and that of Buddha's.

One of the brothers, obviously a monk, suddenly leaned across to his sister the nun and whispered something. She nodded silently, not taking her eyes from me. I looked again at Leanne and asked her what he'd said. It was then the sister spoke directly to me, in a soft reverent tone. 'He noticed you had brought the one who wears a white turban with you,' she said, her body not moving as she spoke.

'He can see him?' I slowly asked, trying to contain my astonishment.

'Yes,' she softly replied, her gentle tone almost suggesting: *Why wouldn't he see him?*

'You will find this is very normal here, Elizabeth,' Leanne shared, smiling kindly.

I was speechless. After one of my daily meditations several months earlier, I had suddenly become aware of an olive-skinned man, who appeared to me in spirit. He wore a white turban with a beautiful feathered jewel. He told me he was my spiritual guide and for some time offered insight and wisdom. Ours was a heart connection, and his guidance a gentle light that gave me strength and reassurance. Initially, I would feel his love and gentleness, then see his face framed by his bejewelled white turban. He told me he was Sumerian. Later I discovered the ancient Sumerians or Mesopotamians established the world's first civilization.

I shared this development with few people in my life, and never with my conservative colleagues. However, within seconds of meeting this family of complete strangers, they simply observed this man with the white turban in spirit, seeing his presence as real and normal. My experience of my unfolding abilities had been powerfully validated. My time with these beautiful people was a huge gift. So too was the reassuring presence of various spiritual guides moving in and through my life, offering support and spiritual navigation. They proved to me that we are truly never alone, even when our earthly experiences have us perceiving so.

8

MEDICINE MAN

Several weeks later, I was called to a hospital ward to meet a young four-teen-year-old aboriginal boy Kevin, who'd been admitted the previous weekend. The nursing staff had written a complaint in his medical notes and wanted me to follow up with Kevin's mother, who was visiting from their community.

Apparently, on several occasions late at night, a very dark-skinned elderly aboriginal man had visited the ward. He'd been seen in the corridor, close by Kevin's room. Visiting at 2am and later, the nurses were concerned that the man might disturb other patients, as it was outside acceptable patient visiting hours. The man and Kevin's family needed to be informed. I'd also been asked to offer the family support, while they were in the city.

So the following day I booked a staff car and visited Kevin's mother at her cousin's house. Kevin had been allowed home on day leave, so I was able to meet both of them.

It was mid-afternoon as I pulled into the driveway of their relative's home. A children's bicycle lay abandoned in the driveway. The front door was open, so I knocked then called out to Leslie, Kevin's mother, to be met by a beautiful face, marked by the sun and life, yet softened by a gentle and unassuming nature. Untamed, greying hair framed her face. Leslie seemed unused to the city. 'The old ways' and her people were her comfort.

As Kevin entered the room, I inquired about the elderly man who'd been seen late at night on the ward. There was a hesitation. Leslie's head dropped, then her hair slipped ever so slightly across her cheek, almost covering the corner of her mouth. She smiled and laughed shyly, her eyes surveying the ground in front of her. 'Oh ... he's from up there,' she began.

'You mean he was visiting Kevin from your community?' I asked, trying to piece together the information.

For some reason, she seemed reluctant to say anything more. 'Yeah ... kind of,' she continued, now smiling at Kevin, who was listening quietly from the armchair across the room.

'I don't like him coming to see me,' he said more seriously.

His mother pushed her hair back from her face and laughed. It was then she explained who this man was, and why he had been seen so late in the hospital ward.

It transpired that the elderly aboriginal man was a medicine man from her tribal community. My attention was immediately captured, and I sat quietly and listened. 'He was making medicine to help Kevin get better. That's how it's done up there,' she shared in a gentle, humble way.

'Okay. So you mean he was visiting Kevin here, to give him some tribal medicine?' I asked naively.

'Nah, not really,' she continued, looking at Kevin and laughing nervously. 'He wasn't really here. He just sends himself here, ya know?' she said, as a chill ran gently across my back.

I felt a sudden surge of knowing. Here was a way of living that had existed and thrived for thousands of years, a level of spiritual ritual and understanding that was ordinary to Leslie's tribal community, but possibly skills we city dwellers had lost. 'So you mean that the medicine man from your community can send himself to another location without physically leaving there? And that's how he was seen on the ward so late, because he actually wasn't in the hospital at all?' I asked, trying to rein in my growing enthusiasm.

Once again Leslie began to chuckle, the rolls of her stomach jiggling delightfully. Kevin was clearly uncomfortable with these ancient tribal beliefs. 'Yeah, and I can hear his tapping sticks. They wake me up at night. That's when I know he's here. This afternoon when I was asleep in bed, I could hear the tapping sticks ... they come into my head,' he said with a sullen face.

'What happens when you hear them Kevin?' I gently inquired, not knowing how long I had before the conversation came to a close.

'I have to go out in the backyard and stand there until I stop hearing them,' he said.

'I hear them at the hospital too. I don't like it.'

His mother gently laughed again. She seemed amused at her son's inability to traverse the huge divide between traditional cultural practices and westernised ways. Perhaps when he was older, Kevin would have a greater acceptance of his heritage, with its powerful wisdom and traditions. For now though, like any teenager, he was finding his way forward in a world that was often challenging and complex.

Kevin had been living in the city with his extended family, while his mother and some of his sisters had remained in their community. Leslie explained that he didn't want to stay with them anymore, so he had come to live with her cousin. This is where he had been involved in the car accident and our paths had collided.

A late-afternoon breeze had blown up, as I left to return to the hospital. As I drove down the freeway, I couldn't help returning to our conversation. Like my experience with the Buddhist family, the information seemed so enriching, so validating and powerful to hear.

It wasn't long before the team psychologist heard about my abilities through the staff grapevine. She approached me about my insights and experiences, sharing with me her own interest in the more spiritual aspects of life. She too had witnessed several inexplicable paranormal experiences, and felt there were things beyond our limited scientific understanding. Before our meeting ended, she requested I not mention her interest or experience to anyone, as she was convinced she'd lose her job at the hospital.

Within days of our meeting, I woke one morning from another dream. I had been walking down a quiet street in an ancient Middle Eastern city. It was evening and I seemed to be in biblical times. I came upon a group of people and was drawn towards them. There was a man sitting at the front of the small group, with a woman directly behind him, her hand on his shoulder. As I approached, the woman suddenly reached over and took my left hand, placing it upon the man's shoulder. She looked deep into my eyes and, at that moment, I received the message: *You can do this too.*

Immediately, I began to feel a powerful energy sensation running down my left arm, flowing into my left hand. Next I felt a tingling sensation all over my palm and fingers. At that point I woke up, with a sense that something powerful was about to occur. I sensed that the dream was heralding further changes.

Shortly afterwards, on one of my days at home with Jessica, I hurried to prepare her for playgroup. Bundling her into the car, I drove across to the community centre. I was about ten minutes late, which was normal for me. Turning the engine off, I slipped out of the car and lifted Jessica onto the footpath, then slammed the door shut on my index finger. Fumbling for the keys, I unlocked the door. My finger was flat and pale, but I needed to get Jessica to playgroup. My finger was throbbing so someone kindly organised an icepack. But as I sat watching Jessica playing with her friends, the pain worsened.

When we finally arrived home and Jessica was in her cot with her favourite teddy bear, I wondered what to do about my injured finger. I felt the immediate urge to seek divine intervention. So I sat down on the floor of Jessica's room and closed my eyes, gratefully surrendering to a higher consciousness—that space of pure love and endless possibilities—asking help to heal the top of my index finger.

At that moment I felt a connection to something greater, yet infinitely wise and gentle. With this came a feeling of expansion into a radiant space beyond hurt or pain of any kind. In this wise timeless place, I could feel a grand yet reassuring presence, a feeling I was touching 'all that is.' Bathed in infinite love, I knew I'd come home to a place I'd yearned for all my life.

The most incredible light energy came flowing down through the top of my head and into my body, then down my left arm to my wounded finger. The light carried with it a feeling of unconditional love, so intense I began to cry. I sat bathed in this beautiful stream of love and light. Tears rolled down my face as I experienced this profound homecoming. When I opened my eyes, the pain was gone. My finger was completely back to normal.

At that moment I had returned to a place of coherence, a state beyond the limiting influences of our everyday life stories as well as the distorted perceptions and emotions that underpin them. In that place of coherence, we can return to our original wholeness, infinite connectedness and deep integration, as part of the divine field of conscious intelligence and love.

Stunned, I poked the wall with my finger and felt no pain at all. Almost unable to comprehend the healing that had just taken place, I poked the wall again, this time harder. There was absolutely no pain or injury. Overjoyed, I broke into laughter. Then I began to walk through the house poking my finger at different hard surfaces in wonderment. Little did I realise, this was just the beginning.

9

A TINY MIRACLE

After the spontaneous healing of my finger, my search for a deeper understanding of life became my quest. I could see there was more to existence than conventional counselling and therapy offered, and I needed to be free to work in ways that were in tune with my expanded experience of life, where I could utilise my new-found abilities. So I decided to begin my own private practice, on the days outside my regular job.

Very quickly, people began to hear about my work. I discovered that by simply placing my hands over painful areas of my client's body, I could feel the same healing energy I had experienced when restoring my own finger. My hands seemed intuitively guided to the energy that was blocked in their bodies. I would then 'tune in' to the areas in the body most in need of balancing, while this loving energy flowed through me effortlessly. Recognising the significant improvement in my client's pain levels and emotional states, I began using this same restorative energy to assist clients experiencing high levels of stress.

As my psychic vision increased, I began to 'see' that imbalances were often caused by an injury the body had experienced during a previous life. To my amazement, I found I could intuitively correct that injury by repairing the holes or other forms of damage in my client's energy field. Sometimes I would be shown fleeting glimpses of when and where the injury had happened. Working within this sacred synergy always felt profound, as it was deeply and unconditionally loving—without judgement of any kind.

As I followed my inner guidance, this new way of assisting my clients felt effortless, as if I were simply remembering what to do. Though I had a degree in counselling, this knowing came from another more intuitive, visionary part of myself. It was guided by an 'unseen hand,' informed by such love and wisdom it was hard to put it into words. The more I trusted, the more my intuitive abilities grew and ... the more I let go of being the person I thought I was or thought I had to be.

The results I witnessed humbled me. I remember Ryan, a young client who had a series of energy treatments for his blood cancer—Non-Hodgkin lymphoma, diagnosed some months before. Ryan referred to me as 'the lady with the hot hands.' According to his mother Sandy, he would ask: 'Why is it that I feel so bad when I go to see Elizabeth ... but when I leave there, I feel so good?'

Remarkably, Ryan was the only one of his group to survive that year, recovering completely. Years later when in his twenties, Ryan would become an international chef.

It was through Ryan's courageous, open-minded mother that I came to meet Sarah, a beautiful two-year-old girl with big brown eyes and a vibrant personality. Sarah had a confidence and wisdom beyond her years. She'd been diagnosed with a rare cancer in her pelvis several months earlier. When Sarah's mother, Jenny, phoned me she was emotionally fragile, yet open to less conventional assistance than was then available through mainstream medical interventions.

I met little Sarah just two weeks before major surgery to remove half of her pelvic bone. This particular operation had only been carried out twice in the world, and never in Australia. Sarah's family was understandably anxious about the impending surgery.

Earlier that morning while at the hospital, Jenny kept noticing the name 'Elizabeth' floating into her mind and was puzzled about it. Later, when she was having tea with Ryan's mother, Sandy encouraged her to call me. As soon as she was told my name was Elizabeth, she knew why my name had been drifting into her thoughts.

She booked Sarah's first session for two days later. Before Jenny ended the call, she told me that after the birth of their middle son, she and her husband tried for years to conceive another child. Then unbelievably, after ten years Sarah was conceived. So she was enormously precious to them.

I arrived at Sarah's house fifteen minutes early. As soon as I parked my car Jenny walked out onto the shaded veranda, quietly explaining that Sarah was asleep. It was then that I first saw Sarah, her little face framed sweetly by her pink ruffled sunhat, her head resting peacefully against the left-hand side of the stroller.

She had just completed three arduous months of chemotherapy and was susceptible to infection. I assured Jenny she would be fine in the stroller. Jenny seemed very relieved. She was just beginning to feel the full impact of the traumatic journey through Sarah's diagnosis and treatment for her rare cancer. 'I've been holding myself together really well through all these last few months, but it seems to have caught up with me today,' she said, her eyes glistening.

Feeling her fragility, I placed my arm across her shoulders, offering reassurance. After a few moments, I looked at Jenny and continued: 'I never know what will happen in these situations. Whatever is meant for Sarah's highest good will be. I never promise anything, because I never know what's going to occur. It's not up to me, you see.'

Jenny smiled and sat down at the kitchen table near Sarah, still asleep in her stroller. I knelt down silently beside Sarah's tiny body and placed my hands over and above her. Sarah was the youngest child I'd ever worked with. As always, my heart felt radiant with love as I set to work.

As I tuned in, I could feel the powerful impact of the chemotherapy on Sarah's energy field. It felt weakened, clouded and out of alignment. Then suddenly, as if travelling still deeper in Sarah's body, I began to feel the cancer itself. I sensed its brutal determination and destructive power.

Both the cancer and chemotherapy were programmed for destruction. There was no peace, love or lightness in them. Pitting aggression against aggression seemed such an odd strategy. It was in stark contrast to the light-filled, gentle, loving method I felt privileged to be a part of. This was a treatment that had no adverse side effects, and it was spiritually liberating and empowering for those seeking its help. Yet again, I felt I stood at the dawning of a new way of healing. I was excited by its potential as an expanded approach to whole health and healing in the future.

Feeling the aggressive personality of Sarah's cancer, I could see it was eating into the pelvic bone itself, attempting to destroy it. Opening my eyes, I looked over to Jenny who was sitting quietly on the edge of her chair. I felt a sudden strong desire to include her in Sarah's healing process, so I quietly explained the aggressive nature of the cancer and how determined and destructive it was. She immediately confirmed that the cancer was aggressive and pervasive throughout her daughter's pelvic bone.

It was then that **we** set to work. As always, I was guided by a higher consciousness imbued with the infinite power of love, which created a powerful healing environment. First, we cleared and balanced the energy field around Sarah's body. Then, without touching Sarah as she lay sleeping, we focused directly on her body, clearing and treating the pelvic area by responding intuitively to what I was being shown. I began to see and sense a large amount of dense energy 'debris' moving up and away from Sarah's body. Then I became aware that this dense energy was trauma from past experience, still held within the cells of Sarah's little body.

As I watched this transformation take place, I came to understand that this remaining emotional debris had, over time, limited the ability of little Sarah's cells to function normally. I was shown that trauma associated with past events is held within the cellular body, impacting the healthy function of our cells. If we're not able to shift this debris and counteract its impact, we're at greater risk of ill-heath and disease. Later, I would reach a much deeper understanding of the origins of illness and how it applies to a person's current life. But for now I was working with these insights as they gradually unfolded.

With lightning speed, my hands moved intuitively across Sarah's lower body. Suddenly, I felt we were drawing the cancer back into one centralised mass in Sarah's pelvic cavity. I was guided to decrease the cancer's size and spread. As we worked quickly, I realised we were deactivating and reprogramming the cellular structure of the cancer, with both love and the highest intentions possible.

Looking back, I now see we were working within the quantum field, the realm of the smallest particles in creation. Remarkably, we were communicating with the cells and, through this, we clearly established the destructive motive of the tumour. By changing its programming and re-educating the tumour, we created a new intention for optimum wellness within its cells.

Each precious moment revealed more of what was possible, as I watched from what always felt was a sacred place of wisdom and compassion, which took me beyond doubts or judgements. In this place of objective awareness, there was only openness to infinite possibility, so the healing process could unfold as it was meant to.

As we finished this part of the treatment, I felt the energy dissipate slightly. Instinctively, I moved back a little way from Sarah and she woke up. She looked around slightly startled and disoriented, then Jenny lovingly scooped up her daughter, holding her against her breast to feed and comfort her. As Sarah lay peacefully in her mother's arms, we continued the healing, directing into Sarah's body an infusion of powerful gentle energy, which flowed into her like a soothing balm.

Within moments, I was suddenly shown a clear vision of a man in a black top hat and tails, driving a coach pulled by horses. I described what I was seeing to Jenny. Delighted, Jenny explained that the family had recently taken a ride in a horse-drawn coach with a man who wore top hat and tails. She laughed and said that Sarah had insisted the whole family take the ride together and Sarah had enjoyed it. As soon as Jenny said this, I realised how symbolic that coach ride had actually been. Through Sarah's chronic illness, each member of her family had been included in this incredible journey of personal learning and spiritual growth. 'So what's next for Sarah from this point?' I asked, knowing I'd be leaving soon.

Jenny explained the next step for Sarah was major surgery, scheduled for two weeks later. It was surgery that had never been performed in Australia before. The surgeon had trained overseas and had performed the surgery twice before. Though anxious, Jenny trusted that surgery was the best course of action for Sarah. The operation would take eight hours. There was a possibility Sarah could lose her leg. I could only imagine how things were for this family, living through their worst nightmare. Giving Jenny a warm hug and leaving Sarah with my love I left, agreeing that I would visit again in two days' time.

Sarah was wide-awake and full of life and energy on my return. Delighted to see her so effervescent, I suggested that perhaps we could try another breastfeed, to keep her still for the next healing treatment. She then watched intrigued, as my hands danced around her. During the healing, she would often grab at my hands playfully or reach out with her bare feet to interact. This time, the healing was a delightful experience for Sarah, as she was so wide-awake. There was a real sense of love and connection flowing between the three of us.

I felt an enormous wave of energy debris clear from Sarah's body. My body began to shake with the power and intensity of it, as the dense energy debris in Sarah was released through me. This energy travelled back to the greater field of energy that surrounds us, experiencing its own positive transformation as it went.

Sarah's major surgery was scheduled for the following Friday. On the Thursday evening, while sitting with my daughter Jessica waiting for her to fall asleep, I found myself moved to carry out a distant healing on Sarah. Once again my hands moved intuitively with love and high intent, while connecting to the expansive, limitless energetic field around us.

Several days later, I received an unexpected call with news about Sarah. Remarkably, her operation had only taken three hours and forty-five minutes, instead of the expected eight hours. The surgeon had walked from the operating theatre shaking his head. He was able to just reach in and lift the tumour out of Sarah's pelvis. It had somehow moved into one central mass, enabling him to remove it more easily. Half of Sarah's pelvic bone had been removed as was expected, due to the damage already caused by the cancer. But thankfully, her leg had been spared. Sarah's recovery was progressing better than expected, and was already ahead of where they'd previously thought she would be at this early stage. Jenny had asked her friend Sandy to call me with this wonderful news. She was thrilled and grateful for all that had unfolded.

Sarah's presence in my life had been the catalyst for significant personal learning. No matter what the outcome of my client's healing process, it was not for me to claim responsibility for it, great or small. I had to remind myself that my only role was to show up in service to a higher loving power, to be an instrument without attachment to any outcome, to remain open and without judgement to the transcendent process of a client awakening in their own way. The more I stayed outside of the equation, the easier and more fluid it became to work with this higher, loving force and its infinite power. The more I learnt to live without my own preconceived notions of how things could or would be, instead opening up to the infinite possibilities available through this higher loving force, the more extraordinary my life became.

10

AN ANGEL
ASSISTS ME

Alongside my private practice, I was still working within the conventional medical setting. When I met with the team psychologist and spoke about incorporating my heightened intuitive and perceptual abilities in my therapeutic work, she was open and interested. As I detailed some of the deeper hidden causes of my clients' physical ill health or emotional challenges, she was very supportive. Before long she referred a client to me, after she'd exhausted all possible avenues of conventional cognitive-based therapy.

I met with Philip several days later. He had been told my approach honoured the spiritual dimensions of life, and was a more expansive therapy and healing. Philip was a harrowed-looking man in his late thirties. His dull eyes, burdened shoulders and clasped hands spoke of a joyless life. Philip seemed depressed and flat. He'd already been to several medical specialists whose results were inconclusive. A clinical psychologist had suggested Philip consider drug-based options, but Philip wasn't keen to take that path.

As soon as I met Philip, I sensed a powerful unseen presence around him, as well as a significant sense of foreboding. I saw intuitively how it was adversely impacting Philip's ability to function and engage in life.

The reason for Philip's connection to this spirit presence needed to be clarified, understood and released, to ensure his psychological and spiritual health. I needed to do more than identify this presence, as many psychics do, I needed to understand the underlying psychological factors that had given rise to this relationship. My focus was to empower Phillip, by offering him insight as to what had led the spirit to become attached to him, then to assist him to discover what toxic emotional residue and contaminating self-beliefs were creating his emotional, mental and physical ill health. I had come to see these spirit attachments as teachers and illuminators, offering us insight, personal growth and the opportunity to free ourselves from those things that limit us.

Initially, I listened to how troubled his life had become over the last six months. Relieved by my openness, he felt able to share his many paranormal experiences, no longer fearful he'd be judged 'crazy.' Taking a few moments he stared into his hands, then eventually his eyes found mine and he began to describe an ongoing feeling of a presence around him, especially at night. He said this presence brought with it a very real feeling of darkness. Anguished, he went on to describe haunting nightmares, which involved his two deceased brothers. Philip was worried they seemed to be encouraging him to join them in the 'spirit world.'

Philip also spoke of a range of additional symptoms: lethargy, periodic body pains, disturbed sleep patterns, depression and occasional suicidal thoughts. In the preceding months, he'd lost interest in his job and was often unable to go to work, due to his emotional or physical state. Nothing of significance had shown up in his medical tests, so he was no nearer to a solution.

At that point in our session, he stopped and looked at me with penetrating eyes. Then as he continued, I could feel the presence of someone else in the room, to the right behind Philip. I began sharing what I sensed and saw. This unique therapeutic perspective I'd developed sat between psychic and psychological perspectives. The psychic perspective gave insight and understanding to a myriad of unseen metaphysical and spiritual factors that influenced my clients' physical and emotional health, as well as their life and lifestyle. It also offered a 'whole person' viewpoint, recognising the soul and its importance to feeling fully whole. The psychological perspective highlighted past adverse experiences and how they create limiting thoughts, perceptions and beliefs: how certain habits and behaviours were actually products of early life trauma, and how we develop unhealthy or self-limiting ways to adapt to these traumas. This approach offered clients clear steps to release their limiting habits and perceptions, so they could return to a state of authentic power. Each perspective enhanced the other, and enabled me to more effectively see and understand the bigger picture. It gave me a larger vision of their potential, enabling me to then offer them safe passage through life's more challenging experiences.

The relief on Philip's face was obvious, as I honoured his psychic awareness. Emotionally vulnerable, he quietly shared how grateful he was that I could offer him a form of assistance that recognised the many dimensions of life he had experienced.

I gently led Philip in a process to connect him with a powerful beam of white light, and asked him to see that light spreading out to fill the room. Then we visually and energetically 'sealed' the room to create a sacred space of healing. Inviting him to close his eyes and take a deep and relaxing breath, I asked him to look around in his mind's vision and describe who or what he saw.

Without hesitation, he described his brothers. I then guided him through a process to uncover why they had remained connected to him. 'They see me as a source of life, a link to the physical world, because they haven't fully separated from it,' Philip replied. We then examined the underlying beliefs he held about his brothers, prior to their passing. 'As a child, I was always told to take care of them, to be responsible,' he said reflectively. 'They were my responsibility. Whatever happened, it was my fault.'

In two short sentences, Philip had uncovered his long-held belief that he was responsible for his brothers, no matter the circumstances. So, even in the light of their accidental deaths, he still felt guilty and blamed himself. This constrictive belief kept him tethered to them, powerfully influencing his adult life, even though this belief had been instilled in him as a young child.

When I asked Philip to look at the nature of this limiting belief as a colour and shape, he easily described seeing the belief as a spiralling metallic object, which he described as being wedged down alongside his heart. This was clearly a storage point for Philip's shame and guilt. He was still holding responsibility for his brothers' passing. Connected to it was a small stream of energy, an energetic tube or cord, which continued to transfer energy between Philip and his brothers. The energy cord had an unhelpful low frequency, corresponding with the low frequency emotional debris and limiting beliefs trapped in Philip's body.

This moment gave Philip an important insight. He had a sudden clarity around his challenges and why they were happening.

I then led Philip into the next part of the therapeutic process: to release the energy that had accumulated like debris near his heart. With reverence and love, we needed to clear the energetic 'structures' that had been set up between Philip and his brothers, to assure their safe transition to the other side, and to allow Philip to move forward with his life. Aided by my intuition and the loving sacred energy that surrounded us, I began to clear all energetic structures around Philip's heart.

For the next and final stage, I knew intuitively I would need the powerful loving assistance of the angelic realm. So I called upon the higher protective power of Archangel Michael to open a door to the next dimension, and to assist Philip's brothers into the light.

Suddenly, the room filled with a beautiful, loving presence. 'I can see him!' Philip exclaimed. 'He's here, the angel. He's right here and he must be seven feet tall, and he has a hood over his head.'

I was flooded with a powerful feeling of love and light, as the majesty of this archangel filled the space with a profound feeling of love. The brothers were then gently led into a tunnel of light by this beautiful angel. Seated opposite Philip with my eyes closed, I could still see and sense what Philip was seeing, within my mind's vision.

After a few moments and with a calm reverence, Philip said his brothers had disappeared. The angel returned alone. At that moment there was a noticeable shift in our immediate environment, from the light and loving higher presence of the angel, to a darker heavier feeling of foreboding. Aware now of another in spirit form, I prepared myself for what I sensed was to come.

Philip had earlier described riding alone on his bike, when all of a sudden there appeared a figure of a priest sitting on a fence and laughing in an eerie, mocking tone. Then without any forewarning, a sudden violent burst of energy pushed his bike over. Philip fell to the ground terrified. As he looked up, the 'priest' had disappeared, leaving him extremely frightened and disturbed. It didn't help that he had no-one to talk to about this who he felt would understand or believe him. He felt concerned people would think he was mentally unstable.

How often I had heard this.

As we continued, I began to sense the spirit's mounting resistance. I took a deep breath and sensed a swelling of love and compassion that spread effortlessly through my being. This expanded state of love and compassion placed me in the most beneficial spiritual elevation for the next important piece of Philip's healing.

It helped that by now I was in a state of grace. I was reassured of the power of love that came with this amount of assistance and that I wasn't alone here. Powerful 'unseen' beings of light were guiding me.

Once again, I led Philip into the same process to locate the energy cords he had with this spirit, and to source the beliefs that had drawn this spirit who was now attached to him. Philip shared that, during school, he was often teased and tormented by his peers. This had set up the belief that he was undeserving of love, of a life of abundance and kindness. His father was harsh and uncaring, further cementing this limiting script.

Working intuitively, I explained to Philip that this spirit also needed much love, and that he was a powerful reflection of Philip's own emotional needs. With the assistance of the archangel, this spirit would now be able to discover how much love was waiting for him on the other side.

Then, with greatest reverence, I spoke directly to the spirit presence. Sending him my love, I explained he would soon return to the light source with the angel, who had come to offer him assistance and support. I reassured him that there would be no judgement, as he moved into the other side beyond the veil. I assured him that there was only love there—radiant unconditional love. In that same moment, I felt the room overflowing with light and love. As always, the higher intervention for Philip was breathtaking.

Philip described another energy cord as 'a chain from his ankles to the spirit.' So we carefully removed this connection at Philip's ankles, being sure to delicately remove every part of the energy structure, including the deeper memory of worthlessness that had embedded itself in the cellular layers of his ankles. I then asked Philip if he was ready to release the spirit from around him. 'Yes, yes!' he replied emotionally.

Speaking directly and with compassion to the spirit presence, I thanked it for creating this opportunity for Philip's spiritual and emotional growth. I then assured the spirit that, as Philip had received the deeper learning from this, it was Philip's conscious choice now to let go of the limiting experience between them, which in turn would help release the spirit into the light. I once again called on Archangel Michael to assist.

Taking a moment to feel the strength and presence of this beautiful luminous angel, I asked Philip to see the tunnel of light opening up behind the angel. Next, I gently requested Archangel Michael to support the spirit presence into the light. I invited Philip to watch the angel, as he guided the spirit into the light. As he did so, Philip saw the chains being taken by the angel into the light, so they could be cleared and transformed into light.

Suddenly, Philip exclaimed with tears rolling down his face, 'I can see the angel! He has picked him up, and he is taking him in his arms into the light.'

The unconditional love and compassion of this angel was majestically demonstrated by the angel carrying the spirit cradled in his arms. I felt so spiritually moved. Thanking the angel for his assistance and love, I asked Philip to let me know once the angel had fully entered the light and closed the entrance.

'They've gone' he said, moments later. I looked into Philip's face as he opened his eyes, and was astonished at the transformation. The darkness around his face, especially his eyes, had disappeared and his eyes were now bright and glowing. They sparkled with light. The relief and release he felt were obvious.

We were both so moved and humbled by this profound experience. It transcended words. Moments later, I noticed two hours had slipped by. It seemed like less than an hour. I smiled at Philip. 'Doesn't this room feel wonderful? Can you feel the light in here?'

'Yes,' he replied, clearly moved. 'This has been one of the most incredible experiences of my life.'

'How do you feel then?' I continued gently.

'Like I could run down the street and shout for joy to anyone who could hear me.'

It was several weeks before I saw Philip again. He explained he was physically and emotionally better than he had been in years. His eyes seemed clear and bright, and he'd had no further sleep disturbances. He also said he no longer experienced any pain, and had returned to work with great enthusiasm.

Later that week, I met with his referring psychologist. She had received an impromptu visit from Philip and couldn't believe the significance in his transformation. 'He looks about ten years younger and has so much life in him now,' she told me, impressed.

Philip's journey, together with others I was involved with from that point on, fuelled my enthusiasm to continue to work within this broader therapeutic model of health and healing. I began to see how vital it was to understand and acknowledge my clients as spiritual beings, to see that within the deeper layers of their personal challenges were spiritual and energetic dimensions that needed attention. So, assisting them to find resolution would naturally have to include spiritual and energetic considerations too. It was absolutely clear to me now that we needed to understand health and healing as a journey of the soul. The value of old lingering stories also needed to be acknowledged, if we were to heal the whole person.

The spiritual dimension seemed a crucial element in our lives and in our ability to fully evolve. Frequently, this profound aspect of ourselves had been sadly ignored. Lying hidden within the deeper layers of our emotional or physical challenges was critical information that was so often unrecognised. By acknowledging that, the healing possibilities were astonishing.

As challenging as it was, I couldn't ignore these profound experiences that were now shaking the very foundations of my life. Everything I thought I was and understood about myself was rapidly disappearing. The remaining me yearned to know more, longed for an understanding hand to hold, a loving heart to come home to.

Sadly, my marriage could not offer me the relationship I ached for. Was there someone else who would be able to meet me in this new place of spiritual and emotional authenticity? If so, where was that special someone? The more I longed for my deeper spiritual and emotional needs to be fulfilled, the greater my yearning became.

11

THE DARK NIGHT
OF MY SOUL

My husband Mark was burying himself deeper in his work, trying to barricade himself somewhere that felt safe and normal. His property development and building company was where he felt acknowledged and capable. The more I changed, the harder he worked. His work became his means of escape from a domestic landscape he no longer understood.

I was now on a fascinating new journey and I longed for greater depth of emotional and spiritual intimacy. Though we'd done well financially, our lives had lost their lustre. I needed a more enriching way of loving and relating. It was difficult, as I also realised that Mark no longer felt supported. Like so many men, he didn't want to talk about his confusion and hostility. I could see the pain he was going through, but was unable to reach him. I could only imagine how unappreciated and undervalued he must have felt.

Understandably, he couldn't relate to my new abilities or the myriad of metaphysical experiences I was having. This was a man who proudly followed his football teams and loved to shine at social outings, enthusiastically sharing details of his latest property developments and building projects. Mark worked harder than anyone I knew. Even though some of his behaviour and actions were deeply challenging, I knew he was decimated by the loss of the 'wife and family' he held so deeply in his heart.

On the other hand, I was burdened with doubt. Thoughts of dissolving our family and becoming a single mum left me feeling confused, hurt and powerless. Gradually, I began to feel that perhaps I'd been wrong to have allowed my spiritual quest to threaten my marriage and my family. This frightened me into submission. The truth was that I was not yet ready to step forward in a more expanded version of myself. For now, I felt compelled to stay in the safe confines of what was familiar.

As summer progressed into autumn, I took refuge in my new clinical counselling position at a specialised medical centre. No longer seeing any private clients, I gradually lost touch with my spiritual friends. I even returned briefly to the Catholic Church. I discovered that Fran and Toni, my work colleagues on the new clinical team, shared a keen interest in spirituality. Conversations were always meaningful and supportive, effortlessly incorporating metaphysical topics and personal insights with known therapeutic techniques. With each of us willing to be vulnerable and authentic, and interact without judgement, we created a team based on complete trust. It seemed natural to open up and share my abilities and spiritual experiences. Fran and Toni's acceptance of my heightened perceptions were validating and comforting. The three of us became dear friends.

It was through Fran, our senior counsellor, that I heard about a workshop to be conducted by well-known American author, inner-child therapist and psychologist, John Bradshaw. Fran was a highly-experienced, loving clinical mentor, who'd introduced me to Bradshaw's books and therapeutic model prior to hearing about the workshop. I was still not finding any depth of happiness and intimacy in my life and marriage, even though things appeared manageable. Fran's insights, offered from her professional and personal experience as well as from her spiritual wisdom, had been enormously helpful. But John Bradshaw's books and workshop blew the door wide open. Their impact was life-changing and hit with Mack Truck force.

Until this point I had idealised my parents, as most of us do, ignoring the blame, criticism and conflict that had generated feelings of sadness, confusion, fear and shame. While many parents try to do their best, their parenting style is often limited by their own unconscious emotional wounds. This, in turn, creates less than adequate environments for many children to grow up in. Old patterns of emotional pain are passed on from one generation to the next.

From our limited awareness, as parents we often create children who feel they are only lovable or worthy if they attain certain goals. These goals that we unconsciously set up for our children aim to fulfil our own unmet emotional needs. When we are self-aware parents, we stop projecting our own past wounds and unmet emotional needs onto our children. When we have the insight and courage to do this, we ignite our children's dormant potential and emotional resilience. The greatest gift we can give our children is to heal our old limiting perceptions and behaviours that cause us to relate to them or others around them in ways that cultivate shame. By shaming our children, we bind and blind them to beliefs that block their potential.

Our children need parents who can love and mentor them into their authentic power. To do this, we need to parent from a place of authentic power. This is a wonderful journey as we can finally let go of past hurts, and be free to be joyful inspiring parents, creating new generations who are free from the burdens and uncertainties of the past.

So I came to discover my own early emotional wounds and, consequently, the limiting core beliefs that effectively thwarted my ability to realise my full potential. These unhelpful beliefs had coloured my friendships, my marriage and my experience of myself in the world. The message was potent and clear: if I wanted to change my outer life, I needed to change my internal life first.

This discovery was so liberating, I longed to share it with others. I realised that if I wanted to do something and it was not flowing as I had hoped, I was probably being impacted by a limiting script about myself, carried subconsciously within me. Instead of trying to force things, I would notice what feelings or perceptions were arising, then I would go within to seek greater clarity and understanding of the unmet emotional needs at the heart of those feelings. Previously, I'd often get stuck in a shame-based way of looking at life, limiting my ability to achieve and interact with others. So I wouldn't finish off a writing project because I feared it wouldn't be good enough; I'd not say exactly how I really felt to a friend, fearing I wouldn't be accepted; or I'd be overgiving to my daughter, out of fear that I wasn't a good enough mother.

This new emotional intelligence gave me a genuine sense of choice in my life, whereas before I'd perceived I had little choice. I felt empowered in my life, whereas previously I had experienced many moments of power-lessness. I no longer felt the need to control every outcome in my life, but was more able to step back a little and allow life to open, to enjoy moments of synchronicity.

Life began to make so much more sense. I found I could live more in the moment. I could feel the sacredness of trees or a shower of rain. Life was deeper, richer. I was much more effective at being able to assist my clients to discover what limited them in their lives; helping them see what kept them repeating old patterns in relationships; whether psychological or spiritual factors lay at the core of their ill health; or why their career or business were not as successful as they wanted them to be. This approach and refined skill base would become the foundation of my new professional practice.

Seeing how effective this holistic approach had been for my private clients, I knew my clients at the medical unit would benefit too. I began to use very simple relaxation processes and visualisation techniques for stress reduction, together with subtle energy work, because for my clients with their challenging neurological disease, talk-based therapy was inef-fective. Well aware that I was working within a conventional system, I was moderate with my intervention and conservative in my approach. Seeing the results of my gentle energy treatments with my medical unit clients, I organised volunteer energy medicine practitioners to work once a week with interested clients in the community. Integrating any type of holistic treatment into my sessions with clients and their families was going out on a limb.

My clinical counselling team was kept abreast of my findings. It was always encouraging to report that my clients at the medical centre were responding positively to the use of subtle energy work, especially as treatment options were extremely limited for those affected by the chronic degenerative neurological disorder, Huntington's disease. This approach had no harmful side effects, did not require the use of pharmaceutical drugs, and positively enhanced the patient's wellbeing. Results showed slight improvement for a number of clients, better than what conventional methods had been able to achieve.

The slow insidious nature of this challenging disease meant that families especially were often distressed and frustrated with so few options. As I talked with my clients' family members, I began to share the significant success I'd had with the holistic techniques. I introduced group meditation, which they enjoyed and benefited from. Speaking about the spiritual aspects of their challenges provided them with a depth of communication and insight that they found nurturing and nourishing.

One of my clients John, an ex-music teacher and father in his mid-forties, was in a moderate stage of Huntington's disease. He now lived in a hostel and needed hands-on assistance to carry out his day-to-day personal care. It was disabling and depressing for such a young person to have to live in an aged care hostel, where the majority of residents were at least seventy.

When I first met John, he appeared withdrawn and depressed. He lived in a single-bed hostel, closed off to the outside world. With his blinds drawn, his room was dark and silent and so was he. John was supported mainly by his mother, a gentle, deeply-spiritual, elderly woman, who had suffered an enormous amount in her own life through the loss and trauma of this hereditary disease. She blamed herself for passing on the Huntington's disease gene to her sons. Her husband, who she'd also nursed, had died from the disease, as well as one of her two other sons. This family's story was tragic.

Over the course of several months I carried out regular sessions with John, using simple calming energy work, relaxation and visualisation techniques. His mother welcomed this new style of work, and was thrilled with the results. We all witnessed a rapid and pronounced change in John's mood and behaviour. His eyes became clear and alive. He no longer shut himself in his room, but opened the blinds and windows and even walked to the dining room for meals. He'd previously refused to eat. Weight loss is a major concern with this disease, so maintaining healthy food intake is crucial. John began to gain weight. His sleep patterns improved and his aggressive behaviour disappeared.

During a patient review meeting, one of the team neurologists pointed out: 'With this disease, to date no-one has ever improved. The patients always have either a period of deterioration or a period of plateau, but never significant improvement.' Yet John was improving, with the use of holistic intervention. The other clinical social workers were impressed and supportive. So we made the decision to use these gentle holistic therapies with other clients and their families, to assist those afflicted with the disease and those caring for them.

After some time, Fran, Toni and I became more open about the methods I was using. We had decided to document the significant results. During a clinic review, one of the team psychiatrists made a quiet comment to me, as John and his family were leaving the room: 'Whatever it is that you are doing with John, keep doing it! I have never seen him look so good. He has certainly made significant improvements, and with this disease we don't usually see that happen.' The support and enthusiasm were encouraging.

Then the two psychologists, who were directors of the medical unit, called an unexpected team meeting with myself, Fran and Toni. The neurologists and psychiatrists, who were also part of our clinical team and who had been openly impressed and clearly supportive of our intervention and its results, were excluded from the meeting. We were issued with an ultimatum. We were to stop all therapy and even counselling with our clients and their families. I was singled out and informed that all my case notes documenting my intervention had already been removed from my office, copied and returned.

My head of department had not even been advised, which was normal protocol. I had actually been spied on through a one-way mirror between my office and the empty office adjacent to mine. What they were expecting to observe, as I sat writing up clinical notes or consulted on the phone offering routine counselling support, could only be imagined.

A full departmental investigation was being launched into my 'unconventional' methods of clinical practice within the medical unit. Special focus was to be given to the specific holistic methods I had used with my client John. As clinical professionals, we had been placed in lockdown. Our every move was scrutinised. It was extremely threatening. We left the meeting in complete shock, which stirred deep old fears within me.

The action taken by the managing psychologists contravened anything my colleagues or I had ever heard of or witnessed. My clients' families had not even been consulted. They sent personal letters of support for my work. Other members of our clinical medical team had also not been consulted. It was obvious to the social work staff and several other team members that this was a personal attack, and that I was being set up for dismissal.

As my work drama began to escalate, I searched for a deeper meaning to this intense scenario. It was clear that these people didn't approve of what I was doing. Yet on a deeper level, I experienced it as personal rejection. Each day I would arrive at work feeling scared and intimidated. Within several days, I was issued with a written ultimatum. I was to be given an involuntary transfer to work in an aged care facility, located in the southern suburbs. I was to begin work there the following week and was to work under constant supervision—the same level that a fourth-year university student would be given in their clinical student practicum. Again, my colleagues and I were in shock at this directive.

Emotional layers of shame and unworthiness were being brutally triggered. Yet it was the experience of deep personal rejection that generated the most pain. It was a pattern I had seen before in my life, but never to this extent. Feelings of powerlessness and isolation began to overwhelm me. I knew this highlighted limiting internal emotional programming that I was clearly being called on to heal.

There were times when I felt spiritually strong, trusting this was a lesson to let go of something that no longer served me. I tried to believe I would be safe and the outcome positive, but it was extremely challenging.

In an attempt to relax and take my mind off the situation, I sought time in nature. I took rejuvenating walks among trees, spent time in the garden and read a little. Meditation brought me the stillness of mind I really needed, and occasionally I would simply sit on the sofa and watch television. One day I saw an ad for the following day's Oprah interview with a Harvard psychiatrist, who would be talking about people having extraordinary paranormal experiences. In his professional opinion, the nature of reality needed to be re-examined. He believed paranormal experiences were real, and the people having these experiences were normal. I sat on my sofa deeply moved by the synchronicity of this, given recent events at work.

The following day after endless commercials, the Oprah Show began. 'Let me explain, firstly, why I conclude that this experience is not psychiatric, and why these people are not psychiatrically disturbed ...' Dr Mack began.

'Why not a publicity stunt?' interjected Oprah.

'The only thing that behaves like this is real experience ... psychosis, madness is not like that, dreams are not like that, fantasy is not like that,' he continued.

On hearing his comments and courage in supporting people who have experienced alternative realities, I broke down with relief and cried. I felt so validated that this man also believed in a greater reality beyond our everyday world. These words came from Dr John Mack—a Pulitzer Prize-winning author and highly-regarded professor in psychiatry from Harvard!

This was the most powerful, honouring moment in my psychic awakening. In spite of everything I had been through at work, here was a light, a voice in the darkness, offering understanding and acceptance of what I knew to be a greatly-expanded spectrum of what we see as reality. Dr Mack's words were validating and inspiring, and gave me impetus to make the decision I knew I had to make.

Having endured a full month of hostility at the medical unit, I resigned from my position to focus my efforts on my private practice. Within months of my resignation, my former client John's condition deteriorated to such an extent he had to be transferred to a psychiatric facility, where he was heavily medicated. His mother and other members of the support group I'd run at the clinic were angry and disillusioned with the medical centre, and extremely supportive of my return to private practice.

Later however, I was brought more uplifting news. Two years after my resignation, the hostel where John had been living finally introduced energy healing to support its residents. Hearing this brought closure to what had been a very brutal and confronting period of learning.

So I began my new private practice, seeing clients from home and continuing my inner personal growth work. This marked the beginning of a new phase for me.

Just as my life and abilities were beginning to flourish, Mark began to shut down emotionally. Engrossing himself even more in his work, he became more stressed and less communicative, working longer and longer hours. I prayed for divine guidance to show me the way forward.

The following month was the seventh anniversary of our marriage. Mark and I had been together for almost ten years. It became the impetus for me to make the hardest decision I'd ever had to make.

12

MESSAGE
FROM SPIRIT

I was feeling excited. I'd had an invitation to afternoon tea with a friend called Cathy and her clairvoyant friend Pam, who had offered me a reading. When I arrived, Cathy introduced me to Pam and we chatted for about thirty minutes. Pam reached over, took my hands then began to tune into my energy and connect with those in spirit who were guiding her.

She picked up on a move internationally, and felt it would be to somewhere in North America. Sitting opposite, I had such a feeling of sacred affirmation—one of those beautiful moments when we get the guidance we've been praying for. As Pam spoke I broke into tears, feeling so validated. I felt the truth of it deep within my soul.

Then Pam began to receive messages from those in spirit. *Feel the tingles*, the spirits are saying. Can you feel them?' I nodded, experiencing a feeling like electricity running through me. 'Oh, that's good then,' Pam continued. 'It's important you remember the tingling. Hold onto that feeling so you can recognise it. Hold on to it, stay with it. This is what they want you to remember. It's very important.'

My hope was that my future would still be with Mark. I had a strong desire within me to keep our family together. Yet I also yearned for greater intimacy and connection.

I arrived home with such lightness of heart. I suggested to Mark that we see a movie together: *Legends of the Fall.* It took me completely by surprise. As the movie began and I listened to the moving chant of the Native Americans, I could hardly believe what I heard: *Some people hear their own inner voices with great clearness, and they live by what they hear. Such people become crazy. But they become legend.*

My eyes filled with tears, as these words touched my heart. As the movie progressed, I felt such a deep soulful connection to the beautiful, snow-capped mountains of North America. It felt like my spiritual home-land and I had such a powerful yearning to be there.

Once the film ended, we decided to dine out at a nearby cafe. Suddenly, I was aware of the powerful energy of an American Indian man in spirit. He appeared right in front of me. His presence was arresting. I immedi-ately felt such a deep reverence for him as I heard him say: 'I have come to find you, to bring you home.' Yet again I burst into tears of joy, as his words infused my every cell.

Trying to explain to Mark what was happening was lost in transla-tion. The new 'me' was someone he didn't understand. As we drove to the cafe, I noticed the white paint on the face of the Native American Indian in spirit. He was still with me. I could feel the power and strength in his body. His wisdom spoke of the power and majesty of the North American mountains, and the land they watched over. My heart longed to be reunited with them. At the cafe, I sat in a state of wonderment. Taking out my pen I began to write down his powerful message, which spoke of my spiritual awakening and the changes about to enter my life. He'd also talked of a time of greater creative strength and depth of vision.

I felt a rush as the familiar tingling sensation flowed lovingly over my entire body, then collapsed into tears. Spirit had called me. My soul was dancing with joy. I was glimpsing my higher spiritual purpose for being here. This was my heart's longing, as it is for each of us. I had finally come home.

Yet as I searched Mark's eyes, he was apprehensive, disapproving. I longed to share this overwhelmingly beautiful spiritual love I was experiencing, but it seemed almost impossible. Change within any relationship is always challenging for both people. I still loved Mark very much, and I longed for Jessica to have her parents stay together.

The following night I finally told Mark I wanted to separate. As I spoke my well-rehearsed words, I felt as if I was in a dream, and that at any moment I would wake up and everything would be back in its usual place. But life had moved on. I had finally let go of the need to keep trying to fix my marriage. It was now beyond my control. I had done all I could. I now had to move on, to release us both.

Mark was torn apart. Holding him, I could feel a huge flow of unconditional love for him that I had never experienced as intensely before. As I cried with him, I felt such a deep desire to see him happy. At the same time, the relief was enormous. That night I wrote in my diary: *I feel so sad, but at the same time so free.*

Tears ran down my face as I explained to Jessica that her daddy was no longer going to live in the house with us. This was the most painful moment of my life. I wished more than anything that she would not have to experience the pain and sadness of my decision. 'I want Daddy to come home!' she would cry. Just five years old, the pain was enormous. And it would remain in her heart for many years to come.

Our relationship struggled on and off for another year and a half, before Mark and I were both truly ready to call it a day. Unbeknown to me, he had begun to forge a new relationship with a mutual friend who would eventually become his new wife. Once he had found a new platform, stepping off for him was easy.

Our beautiful old home was eventually sold. After several years of meticulous renovations, we had to say farewell to all the hopes and dreams we had built together. With great sadness and a tangible sense of loss, Jessica and I moved out. I will never forget the evening she lay prostrate on the floor, her little seven-year-old arms outstretched in her attempt to hold onto her beloved bedroom, sobbing and crying that she just couldn't let go, that she didn't want to leave.

Trying to find the strength to cope myself as well as offer emotional support and reassurance to Jessica was only manageable one day at a time. My spiritual journey became my focus and strength. Supporting Jessica was, as always, a huge priority. Doubts and feelings of insecurity would continue to haunt me in vulnerable moments.

In spite of the challenges in my personal life, I continued to experience such joy in my professional life, assisting others in their own self-discovery. I was often called in to assist at such pivotal moments in my clients' lives, and would be so moved by what transpired.

Even in our most challenging times, the universe brings people and events to light our way, to remind us of the higher spiritual truth that love is always available. Moments of fear and self-doubt can become opportunities to know and heal ourselves more deeply, to integrate the aspects of ourselves still beholden to past painful experiences. In doing so, we are truly set free. Our love and acceptance of ourselves become our liberation. And that liberation is our homecoming.

13

THE POWER
OF LOVE

One of my more remarkable experiences came when Tina, who had been referred by a friend of mine, requested an appointment for her husband Neil. It was a Thursday evening, just prior to Christmas, when I received the anxious phone call. Neil, in his mid-forties, had just been diagnosed with cancer of the kidney. The tumour was sizeable and Tina was obviously distressed. Neil was to have a biopsy the following Tuesday. Surgery for the removal of his kidney was already scheduled.

I glanced through my appointments for the next week and realised I was already fully booked. I offered Neil a consultation on the following Monday, my scheduled day off, as his health crisis was so significant.

Neil walked into my office in an elegant business suit, shirt and tie. Tina accompanied him. For a few moments we chatted about the weather, just long enough to reassure Neil I was reasonably normal. Then Tina left.

Though Neil seemed polite and friendly, I knew that visiting someone who worked in subtle energy therapy was something out of the ordinary for him. His first comment confirmed this: 'I have to say that I am a real sceptic about all this stuff,' he began. Smiling warmly, he added: 'Before I came today, I referred to you as a tree-hugging hippie. But I can see now that you certainly don't look like one.'

'Oh, that's okay,' I replied with a lighthearted laugh. 'I have had a few people come for sessions who are sceptical, but no-one has ever left a sceptic.'

'Is that right?' he said, flashing a wry grin. The playful tone of his voice revealed his enthusiasm for the challenge at hand.

Then the session began. At first I asked Neil general questions: how many children he had, what type of work he did. As he talked about his children and his work as an accountant, I began to 'tune in' to him, then began to share all I was picking up.

For me, this is often like being shown excerpts from a person's life, like watching a movie using my second sight. As I received the various images, I shared the details. Through my own body, I could sense the emotional debris held in his, areas of past pain. Paying close attention to the detail, I shared the feelings and emotions I was picking up on, about where, when and what had created a number of unhelpful beliefs that were stored in his cells. At times I stopped, to further hone in on details of these limiting beliefs held in his cancer. This enabled me to get a good sense of the cancer's own personality and the underlying psycho-spiritual narrative it represented, that had created this health challenge in the first place.

After a while I stopped and looked across at Neil, asking him if the information I was sharing 'resonated' with him. It was always important that what I conveyed to my clients made sense and was accurate. He looked across at me and slowly replied: 'Yeah ... well, actually you're right. Everything you are saying is right on the money.'

From his tone, I could tell he was perplexed by how I'd arrived at the information I was sharing, and how it could have been retrieved. Leaning forward slightly to adjust his suit jacket, Neil settled back and repositioned his right arm along the back of the leather sofa. He then announced with a wide smile: 'So if I open that door over there, would I be likely to find a witch's broomstick sitting in your closet?'

Neil's joke was his way of dealing with a situation that was obviously confronting for him. We laughed, then I shared some more. As I cut through the layers of Neil's defensiveness, I was moving closer to the truth of how things were for him emotionally. 'I'd like to begin doing some exploration work with you now,' I said finally. 'I need you to take off your shoes, then just make yourself comfortable on the treatment table. I promise my head won't rotate or float off my shoulders,' I continued, providing further lightheartedness.

Once he was comfortable, I led Neil into a calming process where he focused on his breath. Then I guided him through a visual meditation process, to bring him into a higher state of awareness and relaxation, encouraging him to draw in the higher frequency of light now surrounding him, to breathe it in. By relaxing his body and attuning his awareness, I was able to help enhance his connection to his all-knowing higher self, his inner guidance.

Once connected to this higher energy, I was guided to take Neil into the toxic 'story' within his diseased kidney, so he could further investigate and understand the origin of the emotional debris and limiting beliefs stored within his cells.

Closing my eyes, I sensed into the peaceful luminosity surrounding me, in a state of complete trust in what was about to be revealed. Immediately, I saw Neil's kidney as a huge warehouse packed with old emotional debris from his past in large metal drums. I invited Neil to step into this warehouse and see how many drums worth of debris were being held in his left kidney, how much old emotional debris needed to be cleared. Neil paused then responded: 'Mm ... well, there are actually a lot of them, quite a lot of them.' This confirmed what I had already been shown in my mind's eye.

'Yes, okay,' I responded. 'Now I want to invite you to discover the age of origin of this emotional debris. Then share with me what that is.' In my own vision, I was being shown a young boy around the age of seven or eight.

'I can see him!' Neil exclaimed in surprise. 'Ha! I can see him sitting there on his own. He's about seven. And you know what he's sitting on? The mailbox!' Neil smiled as he shared this information.

'Alright. So would you ask your younger self how he is feeling then, sitting there on the mailbox at seven?'

From my higher observation point, I could already sense the trapped emotional debris in the boy's throat—the pain Neil was now beginning to feel. 'Lonely. Really lonely.' Neil's voice had become quiet and reflective. He was beginning to re-experience the emotion in these containers which filled the 'warehouse' of his affected kidney, a symbolic representation of the toxic emotional load in the subtle layers of Neil's own cellular awareness. The emotional pain of this old memory was affecting his kidney's ability to function well. This, it seemed, was the hidden factor in Neil's kidney's disease.

We gently explored the reasons behind this emotional toxicity—what had happened in Neil's life at that age. We then looked at how this played out in his life as an adult—his tendency to be concerned with attending to everybody else's needs but his own. As a child, he'd learnt his needs were not of value. This painful contaminating belief had influenced his life choices, his relationships and personal happiness, and had ultimately led to his ill health. 'Yeah, it's like if everybody else is okay, if their needs are being taken care of, then that's all that matters,' Neil explained.

The majesty of it was that in the moment of recognising this limiting pattern, I suddenly noticed a beautiful luminosity in the 'warehouse' in my inner vision. It was a spiritually-radiant light, pouring in through one of the side windows of the old warehouse. Seeing the immense scope of this beautiful light, I asked Neil if he could also see it or sense it, and he could. This was no ordinary light. It was gentle, profound and deeply familiar. I now knew Neil had to connect with this higher spiritual light, to merge with it and give himself permission to accept its healing power.

As he slowly moved into the light, I could see the impact on his face. He had never felt anything like this before. 'It's an incredible feeling, isn't it Neil?' I said softly, knowing the enormity of what he was experiencing.

'Mmm ... yes, I'm walking within it. I can really feel it,' was all he could reply, as he held back tears.

'Look through the light beyond you. Who are those people walking towards you?' I asked, 'seeing' several people moving closer to him.

After a few brief moments, he tenderly replied: 'It's Tina and my three kids.' He was only just able to fight back the emotion welling within him.

Feeling such grace in my heart at witnessing this moment, I continued: 'Neil, ask your highest knowing why they've come. What is the gift they bring?'

'It's their love,' he shared in a whisper, tears now flowing freely. 'They want to give me their love.'

By now the room was immersed in light, in a love that was so tangible, so incredibly beautiful. All the while, I stood next to Neil, feeling what he was feeling, seeing what he was seeing. It was such a privilege. 'See their hearts opening now, see the love pouring out towards you,' I said softly. 'Feel it flowing into you, so that you can accept this gift of their love. Feel it pouring into your heart, into your body, into every cell.'

A few moments later, I noticed a significant shift in the emotional tone of this experience. Neil calmly announced: 'The light's turned around; it's flowing back to them. It was coming towards me, but now it's turned around and it's going back to them.'

I realised Neil had moved into what I often saw as a point of resistance. Neil's limiting belief that he was unworthy had taken hold again, rendering him unable to accept the love offered him. This was the insidious power of shame I'd seen many times with the people I worked with. The legacy of shame was so destructive it would take great willpower for Neil to counteract it. Yet he was also being given the chance to seize his personal power, to rewrite his life's story and achieve what he truly desired—the healing of his kidney.

This was the moment of truth for Neil. I knew that if he chose to continue to believe he was not worthy of receiving love, he was not going to be able to accept this gift of love from his family. So, again trusting that whatever would unfold was divinely given, I gently responded: 'Neil, I'm inviting you to understand that you have been brought to this moment, this place in time, to make a choice about accepting this love. You are being invited to choose the higher truth that you are so worthy of love. Right here and right now you can, if you are willing, give yourself permission to accept it. This is your true birthright. Would you be willing in this moment to tell that little boy within you that he is so worthy of love?'

Then I moved to stand at Neil's feet, as the energy work was about to begin. This point in his emotional process was crucial. Neil needed to accept the unconditional love flowing to him. In doing so, he would allow the higher frequency of love to flow into his body and transform his past pain. After several seconds, tears streaming down his face, he gently whispered: 'It's coming back. I'm accepting their love.'

As he finished speaking, the energy work began. I gently moved forward, palms raised towards him, as the energy poured into my body, then flowed into his. 'Feel the love pouring into you, into your heart and every cell in your body,' I told him. 'Feel it replacing all the old debris in the warehouse in your kidney. See that old emotional debris wash down your body and out through your feet into a tunnel of light just beyond you. Notice that as it enters that beautiful tunnel of light, the emotional debris is instantly transformed into the highest possible light. See the love flow through every cell. Feel its wonderful vibration. Know that this is also your gift to you, this beautiful unconditional love to yourself. Know you are so worthy of this love.'

As the high-frequency current of energy entered Neil's body through his feet, it then flowed gently up and through his entire body, holding him in a state where his health outcome would be optimised. This high-frequency energy brought with it a blueprint for optimum wellness, which travelled down through the quantum layers of space, the smallest manifestation of matter I work with, through Neil's cellular field. It cleared the old painful memories and their destructive messages held in his cells, restoring the blueprint for optimum cellular functioning and optimal health.

The healing continued by deactivating then removing the destructive blueprint which governed the tumour in Neil's kidney. The work was intense and swift. We were clearing, cleansing and reprogramming the body at a subatomic cellular level. After some time, my hands were brought together under my chin. I felt a familiar inpouring of love, as my head instinctively bowed in gratitude for the sacredness of what had just taken place. The energy work was now complete.

I moved closer to Neil's side and whispered: 'Feel yourself coming fully back to the present moment, retaining that wonderful feeling of love and peace in every cell of your body. Know that you can reconnect with this beautiful loving light at any time. You are indeed a part of it, and it is a part of you. Feel yourself back in the room. Take your time and when you're ready, you can open your eyes.'

Neil's healing process had impacted on him significantly. I could see it in his face. Still too emotional to speak, sometime later he hugged me goodbye. Then he stood back, his lovely wife joining us, standing supportively at his side. As he looked across at me, I felt a powerful spiritual connection had been created by what had transpired. Then he smiled with a great feeling of softness and appreciation. Walking towards the door he turned and said: 'Goodbye tree-hugging hippie, and thank you!'

Within three days, Neil was informed by his medical specialist that his tumour had disappeared. After phoning me with his results, Neil wrote a letter detailing those results and the impact our session had made on his life:

The experience with you has changed my beliefs. I am not questioning what or how this healing happened, but find myself accepting something did happen that I cannot explain. I want to tell this story so that others may be touched by the Angel of Light, Elizabeth Robinson.

Neil's letter confirmed that I was being given the opportunity to herald a new platform for health, healing and wellbeing. For me there was no turning back.

14

MY FATHER PASSES

No-one was as loving, present and giving as my father. In his late sixties, he was diagnosed by a neurologist with dementia affecting the speech centre area of his brain. For ten years, I had witnessed the slow progression of his dementia, which left him unable to communicate.

My mother was his primary carer, just as she had been for her own mother. Her life had taken a back seat since her sixteenth year. Her lifetime dream was to finally enjoy the full richness of life.

Often, I would hold a vision of my father set free from the burden of this brutal condition. Soon, it seemed, my prayers would be answered. My father would often enter my dreams. In one dream I was sitting at the edge of a forest of beautiful tall trees when my father nostalgically said, 'Goodbye old trees.' When I woke, I had a strong knowing in my heart that Dad was preparing to leave and this touched me deeply.

Then one afternoon when Jessica was visiting her father, I took some time out to spend a few leisurely hours writing and researching. I'd gone downstairs to make a cup of tea and was instantly aware of a powerful and distinctly different energy in the room, which seemed to emanate from above. So I sat at the dining table in readiness for what was to unfold.

Almost immediately, a wave of lighter energy flowed over me from above. I merged with it and as I did so, a screen suddenly opened in my mind. I was shown my mother sitting alone in the corridor of my hometown hospital, quietly weeping. She was overwhelmed with grief. Then just as suddenly, the image changed to a vision of radiance and light. There was my father in spirit. He was luminous. Radiant with happiness. His eyes were flooded with tears of joy. He was being reunited with his family who had already passed. Just as quickly, I was back in my dining room. I was left with a strong foreboding in my heart: was my father about to die?

Several days later, I drove across the city to a popular beachside suburb to enjoy a brunch with my friend Kathy. She had also moved away from mainstream clinical counselling and therapy, to offer sessions that were more holistically and spiritually based. She served a lovely healthy lunch on the small wicker table and chairs in her sunroom. As always, the meaningful conversation was wonderful. Then we moved to her living room and began to pore over photographs of Kathy's childhood days on the Isle of Lewis, in North Scotland.

Her father, a merchant seaman, was mostly absent in her early life, so Kathy felt as if she'd really never had a father figure. She talked of the isolation of her life on the Isle of Lewis, the cold damp weather and her mother's depressed silence—the simplicity and hardship of life as she remembered it. This was very different to the spiritual journey she was now on. Her grief over her father's absence clearly lingered, and was in sharp contrast to my joy and gratitude at having a father who was so loving and who had participated in my day-to-day life.

Over a cup of tea, I shared the vision I'd been shown several days earlier, questioning whether my father would soon pass over. As I shared this vision, my sadness became frustration. 'I just don't understand why they even show me these things sometimes,' I began, placing my elbows on the table.

Kathy picked up her cup of tea and held it nestled in both hands. 'Maybe they just want to prepare you, Elizabeth. As you and I both know, things seem to have a special way of happening in their own time.'

'You are right,' I replied. 'I guess there's a reason for everything.'

It couldn't have been more than twenty minutes later when my mobile phone rang. It was my sister and I knew straightaway something was wrong. As she told me that Dad wasn't expected to last the night, my body felt suddenly suspended, bracing against the pain of this news. According to the doctors, he'd had a massive stroke. Dad had collapsed not long after he and my mother had finished lunch, and was now in the Intensive Care Unit of the local hospital. Ending the call, I sat with Kathy and cried. Then I headed home, packed and was on the road within the hour.

As I stepped out of the car, I could immediately feel the winter chill. It was late at night and the street was deserted. As I entered the main hospital doors, the heat was stifling. The subtle smell of chemicals lingered in silent places. At that time of night the hospital was dimly lit, the corridors empty. As I pressed the elevator button, I noticed a shift in my awareness.

My father was a wellspring of love and acceptance. He'd always been there to bring comfort, with a bright smile or a warm hug. When I was sad or challenged, his warmth and love made everything seem alright again. But soon his beautiful loving heart would no longer beat and I wondered what the coming hours would bring. Instinctively, I closed my eyes and took a deep breath, calling on divine grace to shepherd me through each and every moment.

Dad's hospital room was silent as I entered. My sister lay in a small fold-out bed, opposite the doorway. My father's older sister sat dozing in a recliner chair. I stepped into the room and walked slowly through the silence. As I did so, my aunt whispered hello. My sister opened her eyes and sat up, leaning on her forearm. She looked exhausted.

With my gaze fixed on my father, I moved closer to the side of his bed. He lay quiet and still, his mouth slightly open. The sag in his jaw told of his stroke. My heart was filled with love, as I leaned over and gently kissed his cheek. Slowly slipping my hand into his, my eyes flooded with tears. 'I love you, Dad. I'm here now,' I whispered, my voice breaking with emotion.

Suddenly, unexpectedly, his eyes opened wide. He reached for me with his unaffected arm. As his eyes lit up, he let out a cry of recognition, then we settled him down again. Though we were all struggling with our powerlessness and grief, we reassured him he would be alright now and we were all there with him.

How I loved my father. We all loved him. On so many nights he'd attended me in the freezing cold of winter, with barely any heat in our large old house. Whether it was an aching ear or scary dream, he'd sit at the end of my bed until I fell fast asleep again. But here he lay now, weakened and ill. And there I stood watching, unable to do anything but love.

As Dad settled, I suddenly caught sight of his older brother George, who'd died at least ten years or so before. He was standing at the edge of the shadows, in front of my father's bed, a warm smile on his face and a sparkle in his eyes. I knew he was waiting for my father, that he was calling my father into the next world. He was calling Dad to let go, to move beyond the suffering of his depleted body, beyond the fear of dying, to enter into a far more luminous place. What was this ethereal place my uncle knew of? Where was he taking my beloved father? The twinkle in my uncle's eyes and the smile on his face seemed to suggest it was a place of great love and joy. Then suddenly, my uncle was gone.

If I could, I would have healed my father. I'd have done anything to make him better, but instead I had to surrender to what was meant to be. My vision only days before had heralded this very moment. All I could do now was reside strongly in my faith that a higher power was governing this process, and be aware of each precious moment as it unfolded.

Perhaps I managed two or three hours sleep in the early hours of the morning. My sister was already at my father's side when I returned to the hospital, sharing that Dad had had a fairly challenging few hours. She'd witnessed his pain and discomfort and was clearly upset by it.

I arrived the moment he'd finally been made more comfortable with extra medication. My sister left to take some much-needed respite.

With my back to the window, I sat holding my father's right hand. As I stared into his face, he was now peaceful and calm. I began to speak out loud to my father about how special he'd been as a dad, knowing that at some level he would be listening. 'Your coleslaw was always the best, Dad. And you made the most wonderful Christmas cakes and chocolate milkshakes,' I said, my eyes flooding with tears. 'You were always so thoughtful. I so appreciated you driving me all those years to my ballet lessons, and all your funny stories. I will never forget how much joy you brought us. Thank you so much for doing all you have done. You are the most wonderful, caring, loving dad. I love you enormously.'

At that moment, I felt a presence reach out to me. It was mystical, powerful and luminous, and came with the most divine feeling of love I'd ever known. Through streaming tears I looked around me, searching momentarily for its source. Then suddenly, I saw my father's spirit lift from his sleeping body. With his eyes wide open and with a beautiful soft smile on his face, I saw his spirit lifting up, just enough to hover slightly above his body. The exchange of love was incredible. The whole room was luminous. My father's face was soft and radiant. Then, just as suddenly, his spirit gently descended into his body again. At the very moment he was back in his body, a nurse pushed open the door and walked briskly into the room. Had my father actually been showing me his spirit, so that I would understand what happened after the death of his physical body?

Later that afternoon, when I tried to share my wonderment and joy at what I had seen with my mother and sister, I was met with blank faces. Talk focused instead on practical matters, on drug options for Dad. 'His face was so beautifully radiant, and the love was overwhelming. I just know he'll be so much happier where he's going. I've seen George and Dad's mother close by. We are so blessed that they are all here to welcome him home,' I said. But my words meant nothing to them.

Leaving the hospital alone and exhausted, I walked down the street in an emotional haze. My beloved father was dying, and my sense of home and family as I'd known it was dissolving. I knew that with time something would rise up from the ashes, but right then the emotional pain was immense. Sadly, my wider family didn't really know who I was.

This often happens on our spiritual journey, and while we may understand it, it's painful nonetheless. I'd had years of preparation for this moment, years of emotional process work, inner personal development, spiritual growth and healing to enable me to experience Dad's passing from a place of greater awareness. In my professional work, I often sat in hospital rooms with patients and their families, as their family members lay dying. All this had strengthened and prepared me for my father's passing. The familiarity of the hospital environment brought me comfort. Yet I longed for the comfort of belonging that family could bring, but we were worlds apart.

That evening when I returned to the hospital, I found my mother sitting beside my father's sleeping body with tears in her eyes. As she gently held onto the fingertips of his right hand, she was clearly bereft. This was a man she had spent over fifty years with. Now she faced the stark reality of her future alone.

I understood her pain, but the love I felt around my father was a beautiful celebration of his life and transition. I could feel Dad's spiritual joy at being cocooned in infinite love, ready for his passing. In spite of everything, it was an incredible gift being witness to his beloved family who were waiting on the other side to welcome him home. This was certainly not an end, merely an end to his time here with us in physical form, a transition to spirit, and a passage to another existence beyond this one.

Sometimes I was able to separate briefly from the more challenging family dynamics around me, to allow God to show up instead. During those moments of mindful awareness, I experienced the unconditional support of a higher power, providing safety and love, a place of spaciousness and ease, without emotional suffering of any kind.

Next morning, Dad was still with us. Initially, the doctors had predicted he would only live a few more hours, but by now it had been days. We'd moved through the painful decision to cease all further intervention, so Dad was being allowed to die, supported and comforted. I knew Dad would never want to live on with impaired cognitive and physical damage from the stroke. He'd said to me jokingly over the years: 'I never want to end up like that. Just throw me in an old sack and hurl me off some cliff or other. Just don't put me in a place like that.'

So Dad was unconscious and settled now. With the assistance of the medical team and regular medication, he would hopefully slip away peacefully. My mother left the room and my sister and I stood at each side of the end of Dad's bed in silence. We were quietly sad and affected by lack of sleep and the intensity of it all. Suddenly, I felt a shaft of light descend between us. It felt like a luminous bridge to the beyond. I looked at my sister, at the light, at my father and back to my sister.

'Can you see it?' I quietly asked.

'See what?' my sister replied, dubious and perplexed.

'Oh my God, it's the most beautiful light,' I continued, as quietly as my emotions would allow. 'A shaft of light coming down and flowing right over Dad. You can't see it?' I gently inquired. Its magnificence was truly breathtaking.

'No I can't,' my sister said. Her voice trailed off; she was no doubt bewildered.

At that same moment, Dad's eyes suddenly shot open. A look of panic was etched on his face as he stared up through the shaft of light beyond him. With his head straining off the pillow and his eyes wider still, he was clearly reacting to the light. At this point, my sister seemed confronted and shocked. I don't think she'd believed me until that moment.

Intuitively I knew that Dad was frightened and resisting. So I moved closer to him, offering reassurance and comfort. I held his hand and said: 'It's okay Dad. It's safe in the light. There is only love there. It's so beautiful, so peaceful. They are waiting for you, Dad. It's okay to go.' As I finished, his head fell back onto the pillow, eyes shut. He was unconscious, but still breathing.

The following day would be his 75th birthday and, true to his nature, he lived through it. We gathered in symbolic celebration of his birthday, but more so of his life.

Later that night, my mother was standing by the fire in the dining room. My sister was making supper. I sat near my mother. The room was dimly lit and silent. My mother stood still, hands clasped behind her back, staring ahead of her, lost in the thought of her immense life challenge. Hours earlier, she had finally broken down as we walked to the funeral home. Placing my arm around her to offer her comfort, I gently explained: 'It's such a beautiful, special place where he is going. There is only love there. All his family will be there to support him. It will be so special that Dad doesn't have to suffer anymore.' But what I shared had been too much for my mother. The pain of my father's loss was immeasurable for us all in very different ways.

And now hours later I sat by the fire, my mother staring off into the distance. Suddenly the energy in the room shifted. I knew someone in spirit had entered the room. Slowly looking up, I saw my father's spirit standing close to us. I began to cry. 'It's Dad. He's here,' I whispered through my tears. My mother quietly stared ahead of her.

'Go into your room,' Dad said. 'There is something there I want you to have.'

I slowly walked into my room, stopping to switch on the light. I knew Dad wanted me to look in my antique mahogany chest of drawers. 'Which one, Dad? Which drawer is it?' I whispered through my tears.

Closing my eyes and taking a deep breath to still myself, I instantly knew it was the top drawer on the right-hand side. Moving closer, I reached out and slowly opened the drawer. I began to sob. There was my first little pair of brown leather baby shoes. They'd always been a treasured possession of my father. He'd taken them in every car he'd ever owned, frequently telling me how my little shoes were still happily travelling with him. I picked them up in my fingertips and held them close to my heart. As I did so, my father spoke to me once more: 'This is the part of you who will miss me the most. Take them now and walk forward.'

On the following day, my sister and mother left early for the hospital. I visited for a short time then left, deciding instead to take a long walk. I made my way down to the bustling streets in the shopping district, past my primary school. Everything here reminded me of my father. Tears cascaded down my face, as I remembered how precious my father was and how different life would be without him. I found refuge in a cafe on the main street.

As I sat fumbling for my tissues, I felt a sudden chill flow over me—I knew someone was trying to communicate with me. Through the glass doors, I saw my father's spirit standing and looking out towards the street, waiting patiently just as he had always done. Before long, my phone rang. My sister asked where I had gone. She sounded concerned. I told her I was having a cup of tea downtown. She explained the nurses had just told her that Dad didn't have long to live, that he could die at any time.

I was only a block away from the hospital when my sister called again, to tell me Dad had just died. As I entered the hospital room minutes later, death loomed large. There was a tangible sense of emptiness. My father's body lay lifeless, like a door unhinged, unused. I didn't want to stay and be with his body. My father was no longer there.

We left and made our way home in silence. I walked into my bedroom and opened the closet to find my most treasured childhood possession— my long-eared, soft toy bunny, with pink overalls, a lovely comforting smile sewn with big bold stitches, and paws that I'd used to wipe away my childhood tears. Packing him delicately into my handbag, I took the car keys and drove down to the funeral parlour. Then reaching into my handbag, I produced my beloved bunny. Adjusting his long white ears, I rubbed my fingers across his paws one last time, then looked up into the man's welcoming face.

'I know this might seem silly, childish even,' I began, fighting back tears. 'But it would mean a great deal if you could place this under my dad's arm, so it can be buried with him. I would really appreciate that,' I continued, trying to stop the flood of tears.

'That won't be a problem,' he said with great kindness. 'And it isn't silly at all. Many people bring us things, special things of great value to them.'

This was my way, my inner child-self's way of saying goodbye to a father I adored.

The following day as the congregation was settling into their seats, I made my way up the cathedral's narrow circular stairs to the organ loft. Silently calling upon the angels for strength, I told my father I was singing my love for him. Then leaning forward into the main microphone I softly said: 'This is for you, Dad.' With my beautiful daughter and my sister's two oldest girls alongside, my heart filled with love as I sang the words of St Francis' peace prayer from the depth of my soul:

> *Make me a channel of your peace. Where there is hatred, let me bring your love.*
> *Where there is injury, your healing power. And where there's doubt, true faith in you.*

Every word was imbued with everything I wished for my life from that moment. I realised that this was what my father had intended in his visit from spirit when he returned my baby shoes to me: to walk forward and not look back, to stand strong and believe in myself—no matter what.

During the first few lines of the hymn, my sister's daughters broke away, too upset to continue. Gathering one of them next to me, I sang even stronger for us all, in gratitude to the man we all loved so dearly. All I could do was live within a place of higher trust. Now, more than ever, I longed to be a channel for God's peace and healing in the world. My pathway from this moment was truly in God's hands.

FUTURE GLIMPSES

Though I could access that peaceful, luminous place beyond the challenges of my day-to-day life in meditation and when I chose to tune in, my personal challenges often felt immense. Still feeling bereft without my father, and with financial struggles seriously limiting any career expansion, at times I felt stuck and powerless. Being a single mum, while joyous, was an enormous responsibility. Future memories of having a loving partner in my life who honoured my spiritual path would suddenly and unexpectedly appear. Tears flowed, as I felt the comfort and familiarity of their presence and loving touch. With so much uncertainty, these treasured glimpses of future memories warmed my heart.

While sitting in my afternoon meditation, I suddenly saw a doorway of light open up only a few feet away. Then, from within the light, a woman in spirit stepped forward and placed her right hand around my left wrist. Almost instantly, my wrist began to sting. This wasn't painful but rather a message that it was time for me to move on with my life.

'Come!' she declared. 'I have something to show you.' My awareness followed her back into the bright white light beyond the doorway. We moved past nameless faces peering from a passageway, and finally emerged in a vast auditorium filled with people. I realised we had arrived into my future. Standing quietly at the side of the stage, we observed my future-self standing in front of the crowd.

Suddenly, her hands lifted up and she directed an intense energy out to the seated crowd. Remarkably, she was able to pick up information on various people in front of her, as she gazed across them. Her ability to tune into their personal issues, their emotional wounds and their feelings was profound. As she scanned the crowd, she sent out an intense current of high-frequency energy into the hundreds of people in the auditorium. With her clarity of intention, she awakened their potential for health, higher awareness and love.

'Why have you brought me here?' I whispered.

'For you to understand who you are,' she replied.

In an instant, we were standing in the silent, dimly-lit grounds of a Gothic church in Scotland. Huge old trees cast shadows across the lawn. Cars were being parked. People rugged up against the cold were filing down the cobblestone pathway and into the church. Inside the church, I watched my future-self engage the crowd.

'Why have you brought me here?' I said.

'You have work to do,' she replied. 'And it's time to begin.'

Just as suddenly, my awareness was once again back home. The woman in spirit was standing near the doorway of light about to depart. 'I don't know why you bother with me!' I exclaimed despondently. 'Why show me these things? Why do you make out that there's some other grander life waiting for me, beyond this limited version of me that I seem to be forever stuck in?'

The woman smiled, slowly turned and disappeared through the doorway into the radiant light beyond. Another woman, perhaps a friend, asked: 'Was she able to understand what she's come to do?'

'Soon,' my guide replied, as they disappeared from sight.

Sometimes our guidance comes in visions, for others it's a feeling or possibly whispered words in our head that point to the truth of who we are, or which is the best path to take. As we learn to pay attention to these possibilities, even if their full meaning isn't yet clear, they help guide us in making choices. Meanwhile, I was locked in a deep sadness; a belief that I was not enough seemed to linger, especially in personal moments and times of deeper reflection.

I had booked an event several months before. My plan was to introduce my work and create a public forum, where I could answer participants' personal questions and offer individual interventions. At the last minute, I decided to include a mass energy transmission at the end of the afternoon's program, just as I had been shown by the woman in spirit weeks before.

The day of the event arrived and the afternoon session commenced. I began by sharing what the woman in spirit had shown me, which had prompted me to move into this new expression of my work. I lightheartedly shared that this was my first time offering group energy transmission—so I had no clue what might unfold. Trusting in the universe's ever-present support, it was time for me to begin.

I took a slow deep breath, closed my eyes, and instantly felt a connection into that boundless space of limitless intelligence and love. With music softly playing, I briefly led the participants into a deeper state of relaxation and waited for what was to unfold. Suddenly, a luminous shaft of high-frequency energy descended and engulfed me in light. With this light force came a feeling of an otherworldly presence, just behind me. Following my intuition, my hands rose up in front of me, with my palms and fingers outstretched towards the crowd. I felt a powerful surge of energy pass down the shaft of light into my body, then out through the palms of my hands and into the audience. The feeling was extraordinary. Intense. I was being used as a conduit for others to transform, awaken and heal.

Opening my eyes, I looked across the crowd and intuitively began to direct the energy to each person as they calmly sat, eyes closed, expectantly open to whatever was to occur. Moving into the crowd, I found myself working across each row. As I did so, wave upon wave of energy flooded my body. At times I needed to regulate my breathing, to cope with its intensity. Sometimes I was working one-on-one, sometimes with several people at a time. At other moments I worked on larger groups and then, finally, the entire crowd. I noticed the participants' faces, capturing the serenity, warmth or intensity of the energy as I passed.

Suddenly, one woman began to cry. Tears streamed down her face as her head was raised up. She looked to the sky, even though her eyes were still closed. Later she was overcome with a powerful feeling of love, so intense that it was like nothing she'd ever felt before. The experience was profound. And so my new work took flight.

One participant later described a sensation of fire passing through him as I touched him on the back, clearing out the emotional pain he'd been carrying in his heart. Another had a headache cleared that she'd been suffering all day. Yet another attendee experienced the powerful release of a longstanding pain in her lower back. A beautiful young girl, who'd been confused about her life choices, emerged from her experience of 'the light' with clarity about her way forward.

My faith in my path was reignited and I began to trust again, to remain open to new possibilities. What I did, I didn't do alone. I allowed myself to open to that healing, loving force that was greater than I, greater than all of us. When we step into this place beyond fear and despondency, we feel strengthened and empowered. It was time to move forward in my life, to reach more people with my work and to create a more abundant reality for Jessica and myself.

It was then that I recalled my psychic reading with Pam, where references had been made to my future life, work and partner in North America. These correlated closely with many visions of my own. It was then I realised that my father's passing had been a catalyst for me to walk forward and co-create a better life—one that offered greater abundance and fulfilment.

LEAP OF FAITH

Some weeks later, Jessica returned home from school and talked about a student exchange program that her school had with their sister school, St Mildred's Lightbourn—an all-girls private school in Oakville, Ontario, Canada. My curiosity spiked as my mind quietly reviewed the threads of possibility.

Opening an email some days later, I was overjoyed to be offered the opportunity to speak at a significant international conference in the US, to present my work and emerging understanding of consciousness, health and healing. Immediately, I picked up the phone and made a call to St Mildred's and was quickly transferred to the admissions office. As it turned out, one of the girls in Jessica's year was moving to the UK, so there was a place for Jessica as long as we moved quickly.

Stunned, I hung up the phone and was suddenly aware of the weight of this decision on my shoulders. I walked to the bathroom door, where Jessica was taking a shower. I stood there for a moment, wondering whether hockey would be on offer at St Mildred's.

Slowly opening the door, I called out: 'Jessie? How are you doing?'

'I'm getting out soon, Mum!' was her enthusiastic response, amid a cloud of steam.

'You know your sister school in Ontario, Canada?' I began slowly.

'It's called St Mildred's Lightbourn, Mum. There are some students from senior school there on exchange right now. And we have some Millie girls at our school,' she added.

'Oh, really! Do they seem nice?' I manoeuvred.

'Yep! I don't get to see them much, because they're in senior school. But one of them asked me where the art room was, so I walked her there and got to talk a little bit. She loves being here but she said it'll be strange having Christmas without snow.'

Surrendering to divine trust, I leaned a little more on the door and continued: 'Well, you know what? I was just speaking to the admission's officer at St Mildred's, and they happen to have an opening in your year. It literally became available this morning. How would you like to come to Canada with me for a while, and go to St Mildred's Lightbourn? Be a Millie girl? Take a year away and travel around North America with me?'

'Cool!' she said.

And there it was. Our journey had begun.

Plans were made and slipped into place. The letting go and moving on was almost effortless. Convinced I was awaiting a better life, I acted without hesitation. The feeling of progress was enormously empowering. Some tried to dissuade me with stories of their own challenging international moves—the lack of friends, of finding work, the long months of settling in and missing home. But I rose above and beyond every story. With the house and car sold, furniture stored, bills paid and currency exchanged, our enthusiasm was palpable. Nothing seemed arduous because everything was gilded in a positive light.

It was the Friday prior to Jessica's final week of school. My world was brighter, and I felt happier than I had been in years. At long last things were moving ahead. However, there was one person who would feel our farewell more than anyone, whose personal story would change our lives forever.

The afternoon summer sun stung my skin, as I climbed out of my air-conditioned car and walked quickly through the school grounds.

LEAP OF FAITH

I found Jessica and Mia sitting quietly together in the front quadrangle. A group of girls sat nearby, enjoying milkshakes and animated chatter. Mia, however, was forlorn. As I approached, the courtyard was steeped in shadow. There was a deep sadness here. Mia's heart seemed heavy and raw.

Jessica recounted their conversation as we drove home from school. Mia had spoken of her emotional pain, how she felt so lost at times, so disconnected, at times feeling like nothing seemed important anymore. 'It wouldn't matter if I wasn't here,' she said sombrely to Jessica. They'd been close friends for the last several years. 'Who would miss me anyway?'

Jessica told Mia she would miss her enormously. 'I told her I would be so sad if anything happened to her,' she told me later, as we sat talking in the car.

Jessica had talked for some time of her increasing concern for Mia. Her parents were successful working professionals. I was friends with her father especially, a well-respected medical specialist and a very caring, outgoing, spiritual man. Mia was the youngest of three children. Her low self-esteem was significant. Jessica's concern for Mia became more evident the closer they became. Right now, knowing she was leaving school for Canada, Jessica felt a strong desire to make sure Mia knew exactly how much she cared and that the distance between them would never affect their friendship.

Several years later, Jessica would share with me something else that had occurred, a crucial piece of conversation that had gone something like this: 'Mia, you have to pinkie-promise me that if you ever feel that way you will call me, or email me. It doesn't matter where I am or what time of the night it is. Just promise me you will call so we can talk, so that I can be there for you.' Pinkie-fingers entwined, the promise was set.

In no time at all, Jessica's final day of school arrived. We said goodbye to the teachers and students, the people who had been our family and home for the last eight years. It was a tearful farewell, despite my obvious enthusiasm for our journey ahead. Yet I knew without any doubt that our destiny was to be in North America. Everything was waiting for us there:

89

our new house, opportunities to expand my work, financial freedom, new friends, abundant opportunity for Jessica, a loving partner and loving home. It was beautiful, special. I already knew this from the glimpses of tender moments that my future memories had revealed. It was as if the gate was finally open. A new life awaited us. I could taste it and feel it.

MEETING
JOHN MACK

When we flew into Canada, a snowstorm had just begun. Everything was blanketed in white, breathtaking and utterly foreign. Within a week, the temperature had dropped to 38 below freezing. A generous realtor drove us to see some rental properties in Oakville, a small, picturesque town southwest of Toronto, as Jessica's school was located nearby in Old Oakville. The scenery was enchanting. The beautiful homes and old trees that lined the snow-covered streets were still adorned with Christmas lights. Built at the edge of beautiful Lake Ontario, this was to become our new home—for now.

The school community warmly welcomed Jessica and me. Within weeks, I surrendered the tedious search for rental accommodation, letting go of the urgency I felt about getting settled. Within days, the universe showed up without effort. I was offered short-term accommodation right next door to the school, in a beautiful old two-storey home due to be torn down the following year to make way for the school parking lot. For the next few months of winter, I could lease the place month-by-month from the school for a reduced fee. Being next to the school meant that Jessica had only a short trudge through the snow to attend classes. This was a short-term opportunity created in heaven!

The following month saw my next hurdle—leaving Jessica behind when I went to speak at the conference in Nevada. She was constantly in my thoughts, though we now had good back-up for her in place. When I arrived, the hotel reception was buzzing with conference attendees checking in, some of whom had flown in from as far as Russia and the UK. The atmosphere was exuberant. My presentation on significant client case studies, using my multi-sensory abilities, personal metaphysical experiences and energy medicine, was scheduled right before Professor John Mack of Harvard University. I was humbled to be on the program next to such an internationally-recognised speaker. As I stood on stage and looked down into the crowd, seated in the front row was Professor Mack himself. I smiled warmly, aware of sudden anxiety. But within moments, all else was forgotten and my presentation began.

Once I finished my talk, there was an opportunity for questions from the audience. People immediately began to move from their seats to stand in a queue at the microphone. Person after person spoke of their interest in my work and abilities. The feedback seemed to indicate I had been well received. As each person spoke, I was also able to tune in and offer personal insights and information. It was always my joy to share and lead others to a greater understanding of themselves or their world. As people applauded, I thanked the audience for attending and walked off the stage.

One of the tech crew moved forward to remove my microphone and receiver and said: 'I thought your talk was very interesting, Elizabeth. From the response out there it seems people liked it.'

'They sure did!' exclaimed Terry, one of the conference organisers, as she strode towards me. 'I've come to escort you out of the auditorium.'

'Really? Why's that?' I asked.

'They liked you and are waiting for you. If I don't help you get through that crowd, you will never make it out. So just follow me. Stay close!'

Before I knew it, the door was open and a crowd of people moved forward trying to get my attention. Many questions were being asked.

Some attendees even threw their business cards over the top of those closer to me. I'd no idea where to look, or how to cope with so many people at once. 'Just keep walking, Elizabeth!' Terry advised from beside me. 'They will follow you, so just keep walking.'

Once outside the auditorium, the crowd became more manageable. Of those remaining, many were unwell. Some had cancer and were searching for insight and clarity about their life issues. They asked how they could schedule an appointment. Others waited in line, wanting to share their personal experiences with someone they felt might understand.

As the crowd dispersed, one woman approached and introduced herself. She was tall and thin with long blonde hair, and had a warmth and soulfulness that was deeply familiar. It turned out she was well-respected astrologer Clarisa Bernhardt, a friend of Shirley MacLaine. Clarisa offered to escort me back up to the main foyer and away from the crowd. She'd been watching me take time for every single person, and realised I needed some respite.

Once there, she suggested a number of people who would be 'good for me to meet.' These included documentary filmmaker Brit Elders, also at the conference. Meeting Brit was a wonderful experience. I was so touched by everyone's generosity and support. It was as if I'd finally come home. What an extraordinary feeling it was to be with people who actually saw me as the person I'd always felt I was inside!

Late morning on the following day, I walked into the large foyer of the auditorium, where I'd agreed to give another short lecture during the lunchtime break. Expecting a handful of people to show up, I was surprised to find attendees snaking all the way around the foyer from the entrance to the auditorium. I wondered who they were lining up for, then realised it was me. By the time I walked out onto the stage, the crowd had swelled to over 500.

Sharing interesting case studies of significant results I'd had with clients, I wanted to take the audience deeper into the infinite possibilities of this new holistic approach to health and healing. It was a pleasure to talk about what I'd learnt about the nature of disease, and how buried pain takes up residence in our cells creating dis-ease. Then I went on to talk about the multi-dimensional influences available to us, to help us access greater insights into limiting patterns and toxic beliefs; the resulting healing it offers; and how I was able to access this through my multi-sensory abilities. I shared how my en masse energy transmissions had been introduced to me by my encounter with a woman in spirit. Then I asked for the lights to be turned down. It was time to offer the crowd firsthand experience.

Afterwards, Liliana Cerepnalkoski MD, a medical researcher from southern California, was first to the microphone. She bravely declared: 'I would firstly like to say that I am trained as a physician and a scientist. During the healing, Elizabeth walked up and placed her hand on me. She pinpointed the exact location of the area I have had a problem with for quite some time. I felt her energy as she approached, and I felt a positive change when she left. I actually believe in this type of ability. We will hear more about energy healing in the future. Thank you.'

Later I would discover that she was a professional associate of Dr. John Mack, who had also come to my event. She would tell me that during the en masse healing, John had felt so relaxed he instantly fell asleep, then woke up refreshed at the end of the healing.

The next person to share his experience was a scientist, who had spoken previously at the conference. He also spoke specifically of my accurately pinpointing and influencing the longstanding problem he had with his left knee. His knee had immediately become more flexible. The experience left me feeling affirmed and grateful that I'd been given a glimpse into the healing potential available to us.

Later that afternoon, I received a message to contact Professor Mack. Though there were no contact details, the person said he felt John and I were meant to meet. Late the following morning, I was on my way to the cafe when I heard a voice. 'Oh! Elizabeth! I'm glad I found you. How are you?' It was Professor Mack, insisting I call him John. 'I don't really do that whole formal thing. Anyway, I felt we needed to meet and talk ... so will you be at the dinner this evening? I enjoyed your presentation by the way. I made reference to it at the beginning of my talk. I don't know if you heard me ...' he continued enthusiastically, which I would come to know was typical of John's personality.

'John, I'm so sorry I didn't get to hear that part, but I really appreciate your feedback,' I stammered.

'Oh well, that's okay,' he quickly replied.

'It was only because I was busy with attendees after my talk,' I explained awkwardly.

'Yes I saw that,' John said lightheartedly. 'They were equally impressed.'

'Thank you for being so kind, and I will be at the dinner tonight.'

'Okay, great. Well, we can catch up then and talk some more.'

The conference dinner was another opportunity to network and connect. John and I and other guest speakers shared a table. We all enjoyed sharing insights and experiences. It was wonderful. However, it wasn't until the week after I arrived back in Ontario that John's secretary called. 'John would like you to come down to Boston for the opening night of a new documentary film he's in. There will be a number of people flying in, people he feels it would be good for you to meet, so he asked me to call and invite you personally. He also said that he expects you will stay at his home in Cambridge. There will be a number of people staying. It's a large home and has ample room for everyone.'

I was almost unable to reply. There was simply no way I could stay at John's home with 'significant others'. 'I would be honoured to be at the opening night. Please let John know I will be there. But I simply couldn't stay at John's home. So I will book a hotel close by.'

'John specifically asked me to let you know that there will be a room for you. It's all arranged. He has a number of other guests staying. This is something he does often, so you don't have to worry,' she shared, trying her best to reassure me.

'I really appreciate the invitation, but I just couldn't possibly stay,' I replied, sounding stressed, struggling with the 'I'm not good enough' and 'I'm not worthy enough' stuff.

As I held my ground, she finally said she would let Professor Mack know I wouldn't be staying. 'I'm sure he will be disappointed, but I will let him know.'

John phoned himself the following morning. 'What's all this about you not staying? I've arranged everything. It's very simple. It will be good for you. So don't fuss, okay? Just stay here in my house. There will be others staying. It will be good for you to meet them, so that's why I want you here. It's a large house with several floors and a number of rooms, a very comfortable home. Anyway, you will see when you get here. You will have your own room, but will have to share the bathroom on the top floor. So it's all arranged. I'll see you Friday.' And with that, the conversation ended.

It was several days after the opening night of the film, and the house guests had all but gone. I made my way downstairs, and found myself alone in the large comfortable kitchen, where the fire was burning warmly, *The Boston Globe* and *The New York Times* had been left well read at the end of the kitchen table. I reached up and chose a blue-green pottery mug for my morning cup of tea, then felt a cool wave of chills as I noticed the initials 'ER' in the bottom of the mug. I felt a sudden deep feeling of home.

Some hours later, I browsed the shops in Harvard Square. As I stared at the watches in a jewellery store window, time seemed to shift—and with it came a feeling that I was now home and living here. Right at that moment, snowflakes crystallised in the air and it began to snow. And I began to cry.

Back at John's house later in the day, Dr Liliana Cerepnalkoski phoned to tell me that during my healing event at the recent conference, she had experienced the opening of her own latent intuitive and energetic abilities, and had embarked on a research study of intuitive and energetic medicine, comparing various traditions from around the world. I strongly encouraged Liliana in her explorations, as I'd received clear visions of her potential and power. I could see her becoming internationally known in the fields of medical intuition and energy medicine, with her work eventually making significant contributions to the emergence of a new paradigm of health and healing.

The following day, while having morning tea with another local author in the holistic health field, I was encouraged to move to Cambridge, to be in a more supportive community. She invited me to visit her home several streets away, suggesting I could temporarily rent her ground floor apartment.

John offered to drive me over to her house. On the way, he asked why I was visiting. When I explained, he came back with: 'Well, if you are moving here—and I think that is a very good idea—it would be better for you to stay at my house. You can have the rooms upstairs on the third floor. I'll see you back at the house later.'

Within two weeks, we'd packed up the house in Oakville and stored some of the furniture I had brought. Once again, Jessica said goodbye to her school friends. She seemed relieved. She had found the new school challenging in many ways.

We arrived at John's house in Boston in the early afternoon. It was a warmer March day, and recent snow had melted. The crisp breeze, however, reminded us winter wasn't over. Yet there was a sense of real possibility here. The taxi pulled up on the sidewalk at the bottom of the stairs to John's front door. Within moments, John appeared with such a joyful expression, welcoming us with great affection. We felt immediately at home.

With our luggage finally inside, John took us on a tour of his beautiful home, which was once the residence of famous American composer and songwriter, Cole Porter. We climbed the stairs to our bedrooms on the third level. It all felt divinely scripted. John's house was home to many. He would have guests coming and going, almost every few days. We were constantly meeting new and interesting people, or preparing afternoon tea for local friends and neighbours.

Life with John was inspiring and always deeply nourishing. He encouraged me and was open and interested in all I could see and do. The multi-dimensional world I lived in was a source of subdued fascination for John. Yet he always remained open and inquiring with a well-trained academic eye.

Very quickly, we became like family. John would playfully tell Jessica we were related by 'house.' He would often sit and practise at the baby grand piano, just off the kitchen downstairs. Very youthful at 73, he had recently taken up piano lessons. Unbeknown to him, Jessica would creep past the hallway door into the kitchen, then across to the other side of the room where the kitchen opened into the dining room, just behind the piano. She would silently stand there and unexpectedly clap and cheer as he ended the piece he was playing. It was such fun. Mostly, I would cook and John would eat with us if he was home. It was a special experience of connection and belonging for Jessica and I, a gift I would forever treasure.

The most significant part of this new community was that they were open and interested in my world, and in the way I saw and sensed things. Living in a home and community, where those close to me accepted and valued who I was, made John's house seem like home. It was in sharp contrast to the life landscape I had been struggling with prior to leaving Australia. Taking a great leap of faith to follow my spiritual calling to North America, together with the many synchronicities and luminous stepping stones I'd experienced, had led me to a place where I felt spiritually liberated and personally validated.

The place where I then was, the people I was mixing with, and the possibilities before me felt fully aligned—as if the divine and I had dreamt it into reality. So I remained open and grateful, asking for clarity of purpose, trusting I'd take the right step each new day.

SETTLING INTO
BRATTLE STREET

While enjoying a leisurely breakfast one morning, I tuned into someone visiting in spirit, standing at the end of the table. It was a woman who used to love to sing, who was connected to John's grand piano. Somewhat amused, John realised it must have been his great aunt, who once owned the piano. He walked over to the kitchen counter, made himself another cup of coffee and listened to me share his aunt's message.

Suddenly he stopped and stared out the window into the garden. 'That's who I need to introduce you to. She will enjoy you,' he said, as he turned and walked towards the door.

'Who would that be, John?' I asked.

'Shirley MacLaine. Remind me will you?' he said, as he glanced back towards me.

'Remind you to do what, John?' I replied.

'To introduce you to her,' he said as he disappeared.

The following week John was away. He had been invited to a very beautiful country retreat for writers outside Boston, to focus on one of his literary projects. The house seemed empty while he was gone. On his return, Jessica and I threw open the front door, and ran down the front stone steps and onto the sidewalk, glad to see his radiant smile. Life had returned again to the house.

Within the month, we drove north to John's home in exquisitely beautiful woodland, in the heart of Vermont. Old grandfather maple trees graced the driveway. We had our first glimpse of John's historic two-storey house, built in the 1850s at the top of a hill. Down below, a large pond offered refuge for wild geese and ducks.

After a long walk in the woods through John's magnificent property, we enjoyed dinner at a local restaurant, then returned home to settle in for the night. With Jessica asleep, I made some tea and looked into the sitting room, to check in on John. He'd made a cosy fire and was seated in one of the two old armchairs to the right of the fireplace, glasses perched on his nose. For a fleeting moment, I recalled the day I had watched him on Oprah some years before, speaking about his latest book. It had been my first introduction to John and his work. He'd appeared at a time when I needed validation. And yet never did I consider I would be a guest in John's family home.

'Am I disturbing you, John?' I quietly asked.

'No, come in. Come and sit down,' he replied, as he moved a throw rug from the seat opposite and tossed it onto the sofa nearby.

'I've made you a hot cup of tea,' I said, as I placed his cup down on the small table beside him and seated myself in the chair opposite.

The glow of the fire beckoned. Staring into it soothed my mind, drawing me into contemplation. As usual, the moment drew us into meaningful conversation. John began sharing more of his new avenue of research into the life and afterlife of notable American psychiatrist and researcher, Dr Elisabeth Targ. Elisabeth was the daughter of well-known author and physicist Russell Targ, a pioneer in the development of the laser and co-founder of Stanford Research Institute's investigation into psychic abilities in the 1970s and 1980s. Elisabeth was raised in a family where extrasensory perception was encouraged and researched. She completed high school at just fifteen and later graduated from Stanford Medical School, completing her residency at UCLA. Her research into the effects of prayer on disease gained her the attention of the wider community and national media. Later her promising results and pioneering work were given major funding, and Elisabeth began her study into the effects of distant healing on the rarest and the most aggressive form of head tumour: glioblastoma multiforme.

Incredibly, during the trials of this study, Elisabeth began to experience neurological health problems, which led to a shocking discovery. Elisabeth was diagnosed with head cancer—the exact malignant, aggressive form of cancer she had been called to study. Tragically, despite many people's attempts to heal her, Elisabeth died just prior to her 41st birthday.

Our conversation turned to evidence of Elisabeth's after-death communications. 'The other day you began to tell me, John, about a phone call from a medium in Spain to Elisabeth's husband Mark, after Elisabeth passed over; someone he'd never met and who'd never met Elisabeth,' I prompted. 'You said she knew specific things about Elisabeth that she couldn't have known unless Elisabeth was communicating with her. That's powerful evidence and it brings to light the reality of her survival. You said there was much more to this story. Sounds fascinating!'

'It's certainly a compelling story,' John replied, the light from the fire casting a warm glow across his face. 'Elisabeth's husband, Mark, received a call from a woman in Spain who he'd never previously met. Mark answered the phone and heard the woman speaking to him in very rudimentary English. She made reference to the spirit of a woman who had apparently appeared to her. She explained that she was a medium and worked with the spirits of those who were deceased. She told Mark that the spirit had said her name was Elisabeth. Apparently, Elisabeth's spirit had simply appeared to this medium in Spain, then established communications.

'The medium then explained that there were some words that she thought were Russian. Elisabeth wanted her to make contact with Mark and pass on those words. When the medium described the words to Mark, he recognised them as one of Elisabeth's favourite Russian love songs, which makes sense when you know that Elisabeth was fluent in Russian and also spoke fluent French and German. There are many interesting aspects to this story,' John shared.

'So how did the medium know Mark's phone number, John? Did she look it up? How could she have found it?' I inquired, feeling the haunting intensity of the 'other world' watching on from dark corners in the room.

'It seems Elisabeth had given it to this medium. According to Mark, the woman had just dialled the number Elisabeth had given her. Anyway, I'm very excited by this research. I feel like it will establish a whole new body of work. Survival of consciousness after the death of the body is an area of research I never really thought much about before. But the more I learn of it, the more excited I am about it. I'm flying out to San Francisco in a few weeks to meet with Mark and do some more research. After that, I'll begin writing.'

The fire was burning lower now but the radiant light glowing from John's face seemed to emanate from his soul, from his passion to open up new frontiers and free people from their limited awareness. John's new work was to draw him into the new arena of survival of consciousness following the death of the body.

Moved by the depth of his enthusiasm, I asked John what the personal significance of this new area of research was for him. His face softened and he looked reflectively into the fire saying quietly, 'Maybe it's preparing me.'

'For what?' I gently asked.

'Well, I turn 74 this year. Maybe they are getting me ready to understand what's soon to come,' he continued reflectively.

'But you have so much more to do, John. You and your work are so important here. You'll be here for a long time yet,' I assured him, adding softly: 'In any case, we would all be completely bereft without you!'

'Well, you never know about these things,' John quickly replied. 'We can't go on forever. Anyway, it seems very significant, like things are moving on; a closure of sorts to my other research, like that chapter's complete or something. In fact, it almost seems to be happening in some higher, perhaps even preordained, way.'

John stared into the fire for a moment of reflection. 'We have to remind them,' he said, suddenly more determined. 'They have to be reminded. We've got to change the way people think. That's why you've come here. You see so much. You've had such a broad range of experience, and that's crucial to what you offer. What you have personally experienced is more than many, and this is why you need to be heard. That's why it's so important for you to share what you see, what defines reality as you know it. We have to get you seen and heard. I'll do what I can to have someone review your book project. That's a good place to start.'

He smiled and reached over to pick up his tea from the table. His words were so validating. Even if nothing further eventuated, knowing someone like John believed in me was a true gift.

'But what if people think I'm crazy, John?' I asked meekly.

'Who cares what people think? People will think what they want to think. Sharing what you see and know will make them sit up and question, and that's more important.' With that, he stood up from his armchair and announced he was retiring to bed.

It was strange. I felt more at home here in the US than anywhere in my life. Being with John and the others felt natural and meaningful. Being in their midst called me into a sense of conscious community that I had never felt so strongly before. So it seemed like a natural progression when John suggested I make my stay in the US official. Within days, he encouraged me to speak to an immigration attorney. He was keen to support my living and working in the US, and made it clear that he would do everything in his power to make that happen. John became my sponsor.

Within several months my official papers arrived at the house, declaring me able to live and work in the US for the next six years. 'Forget about Australia! You're an American now!' John declared. 'Just get on and do what you've come here to do. That's all you need to think about. We need to get you out there now. We need to get you seen.' They are words I will treasure forever.

As the weeks and months unfolded, it had become clear that Jessica needed structure, routine, continuity, a supportive new group of friends and a sense of home and stability. Schooling in Boston was a major challenge, but the high cost of renting was even more staggering. I was guided to explore the option of moving to a charming town on the west coast in southern Oregon.

Ashland was a quaint, friendly, small college town nestled in the picturesque Rogue Valley. Every year from February to October, the town's population swelled with 100,000 visitors attending the Tony Award-winning Oregon Shakespeare Festival. Toss into the mix great restaurants, easy airport access and reputable schools, and a ten-day visit had me sold.

Living in Ashland was more affordable than Boston. Ashland had also become the headquarters for authors and leaders in the new consciousness field. This was the home of internationally-known spiritual luminaries like Neale Donald Walsch, Jean Houston, Gary Zukav, Gangaji, Donna Eden, James Twyman and others, whose presence acted as a beacon to the consciousness community.

Even though Jessica and I loved John, and felt so welcomed and supported by him, I made the decision to move to Oregon to give Jessica more stability and structure. Saying our fond goodbyes, Jessica and I flew out to the west coast to our new rental home on Holly Street, Ashland, nestled on a peaceful mountain hillside where deer roamed the streets.

With the arrival of our belongings, I began to unpack and create a home. Magnificent old trees throughout the 93 acres of forested Lithia Park in central Ashland soon turned from summer green to the splendid multi-coloured symphony of autumn. Surrounded by a supportive nest of friendly neighbours, stately old pines and beautiful mountain and valley vistas, our house very quickly and rather effortlessly became our home. The new school year had just commenced and our hopes were high for fruitful beginnings in the months ahead.

SECOND THOUGHTS

Jessica sat quietly enjoying her breakfast of pancakes, with maple syrup brought back from our visit to John's house in Vermont. It reminded us of John. We both missed him. We were planning a visit to the supermarket as soon as Jessica finished her pancakes, when the phone rang.

'Liz, it's Mark,' came a traumatised voice on the line. It was my ex-husband. I knew instinctively he had some shattering news.

'Oh my God, Mark! You sound dreadful. What's happened? Are you okay?'

'Yeah ... well ... I have some bad news, Liz. I'm in intensive care. I'm okay ... but I nearly died. I'm still not too good really.'

At that moment my legs lost their strength. I sank to the floor. 'Oh God ... are you going to be alright? What happened?' I said, breaking into tears.

'Yeah ... I just needed to let you know,' he said, then added: 'I rang to speak with Jessica actually.'

'That's okay, Mark,' I said quietly. 'Just tell me what happened.'

'I had an accident up north. I was stuck in a small country hospital. They had to airlift me out to operate because it became critical,' he continued, with obvious physical and emotional distress.

The shock was shutting me down. If Mark died, I couldn't live knowing I had taken his only child to the other side of the world. 'Mark, how did it happen?' I asked.

It transpired that Mark and his business partner Jeff had been on location, overseeing housing construction operations in a remote area of Western Australia. They decided to try their hand at some gold prospecting and were over 100 kilometres inland of the small town of Meekathara—an aboriginal name meaning 'place of little water'—in Australia's mining heartland. It was early summer in Australia, and temperatures were already climbing towards boiling point.

Jeff had been operating a large piece of excavating equipment and accidentally swung the huge metal bucket of the backhoe into Mark's side, throwing him more than six metres through the air, spearheading him onto the hard ground, where he lay motionless. Their remote location with no phone coverage made the situation more desperate. Mark was critically injured and the closest help was an hour's drive along a dirt road to the cattle station where they were staying. Jeff drove there to alert emergency services and, using a two-way radio, contacted the Royal Flying Doctor Service. During this time Mark lay alone on the dusty red earth in the heat, struggling to breathe. The one thought in his mind was his love for Jessica. He had to live to see her again.

Back at the cattle station it was not good news. The airstrip on the cattle station was not in good enough condition to enable the Royal Flying Doctor Service plane to land. Instead, the doctor advised Jeff to drive back out to the scene of the accident in the cattle station's truck, lift Mark into the back of the truck and take him back to the station. Three long hours after Mark had been severely injured, they arrived back at the cattle station. Once again, Jeff spoke to the doctor via the two-way radio and was directed to give Mark an injection to relieve his chronic pain. Mark would later be diagnosed with four broken ribs and a severely damaged lung.

Jeff ran back out to the truck and gave him the necessary injection, then drove the truck with Mark still in it to meet an ambulance that was on its way. Mark was transferred to the ambulance and driven back to the local hospital, which only had one patient admitted at that time. And that was Mark.

After a week Mark's condition worsened, and he was airlifted to a hospital in Perth, where he was diagnosed with a chronic infection of the cavity between the lung and chest wall. During the ensuing surgery, Mark's liver was accidentally cut. The bleeding became very difficult to stop. His condition was again diagnosed as life-threatening. The surgery took seven and a half hours, and he was then transferred to the critical care unit.

It was several days after the surgery, and Mark was calling Jessica to let her know what had happened and to hear the voice of the daughter he loved. 'Thank God you're alive, Mark!' I responded, still trying to assimilate what he had shared. 'Please take care. I'll get Jessica.'

'I will, Liz. Take it easy. I'll be okay,' he said quietly.

I handed the phone to Jessica, preparing to support her as she received the difficult news.

Later that night after Jessica had fallen asleep, my thoughts lingered on Mark's accident, triggering a stark awareness of the impact of my decision to leave Australia, taking Jessica away from her father and her home. I realised how frivolous it must have seemed to everyone, my taking Jessica away from her father, school and friends, to chase a personal dream of mine and find a 'better life' for us both. Suddenly, the reason for moving away held far less importance. Yet on a deeper level, I knew something of significance was yet to unfold on our journey.

Often when we embark on a journey, having made a decision to take action on a creative idea or plan, we have great intentions, expecting everything will unfold smoothly and supportively. Then, when we experience an unexpected change, loss or challenge, we can interpret our actions as a wrong choice, falling into a spiral of self-blame and self-doubt.

It's important to realise our perceptions are at the root of our conflict here. We often assume things will go according to our version of a successful outcome, believing that if we are on our spiritual journey, the road will always rise up to meet us, bringing us comfort rather than discomfort. However, it is most often in challenging moments that we are given invaluable opportunities to build resilience, learning how best to navigate the challenges and change. So, it's these opportunities to learn that are the true reason for taking the journey in the first place.

Success is often perceived as reaching a desired goal or destination. But true success is learning to skillfully navigate those unexpected moments with wisdom and emotional integrity, trusting that the experience is helping us evolve.

Knowing that every crisis and challenge offer us the opportunity to grow and evolve, I held strong in my faith that I had been drawn to America for a reason. I believed that, with patience and trust, the reason would reveal itself and bring with it the life and opportunity I longed for.

LOVE
NEVER DIES

Life continued in our small Ashland community. Attending middle school gave Jessica the opportunity to make new friends. As the weeks progressed, Mark's health improved. Jessica began to bring home her new friends. I enjoyed their company, but my extra-sensory perception was an increasing source of embarrassment and tension for Jessica. She would often say she would rather I was a hairdresser or 'something normal and not so weird.' For teens it's all about acceptance, so having a mum who did 'weird' things may have made it harder for Jessica to be accepted by her new friends. I really understood that.

Yet many of her friends took an interest or solace in what I could see or make sense of for them in their day-to-day lives. One school friend, Nicole, had an older brother in the army and within months he would be sent to the Middle East. One particular afternoon Nicole opened up. Her family home was in the historic part of town. One day while picking up Jessica from there, I was invited in. I felt a very real presence of 'others' in spirit in the house, especially upstairs. So what Nicole subsequently told me didn't take me by surprise. Her story was typical of my own childhood and that of many others who are able to see or sense those in spirit.

At night while lying in bed, Nicole would often 'hear' people talking, as if there were other people in the room. She could not see these people, but felt their presence and 'heard' their voices. Her older brother had teased her, saying that she would end up 'crazy' like their mother. She had talked to her school counsellor, who no doubt interpreted Nicole's experience as 'abnormal.' Modern psychiatry does not accept the existence of other realities or extrasensory perception, which leaves teenagers like her feeling very alone. Nicole's experience would be explained as auditory hallucinations. Clinical diagnosis would normally result in drug therapy, doing little to get to the cause of the problem.

Nicole had told the counsellor about the 'people' she'd see walking down the corridor and disappearing downstairs at home. She felt confused and alone, as she had no-one she could trust to share this with. Her mother had been depressed and medicated for years. Unfortunately for Nicole, the school counsellor phoned her father and indicated the need for further psychiatric evaluation and possible medication. There were inferences of early-onset schizophrenia.

The phone call left Nicole's father concerned. To diffuse the situation, Nicole told her father she had made it all up. She was grounded for two weeks then life continued on, with Nicole feeling confused, misunderstood and still frightened about what she was experiencing at night.

Nicole was relieved to talk to an adult who'd had similar experiences. I explained that many, many people all over the world had similar experiences, then provided further insight on alternative and empowering ways to interpret, understand and better cope with what might be happening.

Teaching teens to interpret their experiences, and extract wisdom and insight from each life situation, strengthens their resilience and builds confidence and self-trust. Assisting them to cultivate an inner witness and wonderment in the situations they meet in their daily lives is a key strategy for their empowerment. Once they have cultivated an inner more objective observation of the way they're operating, non-judgementally noticing what's arising for them emotionally and why, they can choose to respond differently to tricky situations, including metaphysical experiences.

Working on changing the limiting lens they use to interpret the experience will change the experience for them. It's about shifting focus from: *This is happening to me because there is something weird about me*, to: *This is happening to offer me insight and wisdom about who I truly am, and about what life truly can be for us all.* This new perspective changes everything.

Once they develop an awareness 'muscle', their experience no longer defines them nor confines them. Unexpected situations are no longer fearful or overwhelming but educational, offering greater wisdom and insight. As teens learn to moderate their emotional responses, experiences take on new meaning, and they feel far more empowered.

Cultivating their connection with a higher intelligence fosters trust, and reassures them they are truly never alone in any experience. Equally, learning to call upon the angelic realm reassures them, and heightens a sense of loving higher connection, rather than feeling separate.

With so much misunderstanding and misinterpretation of out-of-the-ordinary experiences, teens can feel very isolated and alone, disconnected from their friends. As a parent, it's essential to demonstrate you understand by listening and responding with empathy and compassion. To listen from a place of non-judgement, rather than criticism, fosters feelings of safety and transparency, and cultivates loving connection.

As a society, when we shift our focus from dismissing and judging out-of-the-ordinary experiences to broadening our understanding of the multidimensional nature of the human experience, we will finally be able to provide better support, understand and provide our teens with tools to live powerful, authentic lives.

When we'd finished talking about Nicole's psychic experiences, I asked her how she was feeling. Through teary eyes she replied: 'Not so alone.'

Nicole's story is not an isolated one. Far too many sensitive children grow up feeling frightened and alone. Instead of understanding that they have special abilities and insight and helping them evaluate what they've experienced, they're left alone to face their personal challenges. This makes it hard for them to build the necessary resilience to be truly empowered, insightful teenagers, who happen to have special gifts.

As I came into contact with more local teenagers through Jessica, it seemed our move to this small town was meant to be. Coming to know these very special young people really highlighted how much society needs to step free from our limiting view of ourselves and our world, to embrace a broader vision of reality. This reality has numerous intricate layers which, when harnessed, can have a profound impact on health and wellbeing. Imagine how different things would be if we were to teach these young adults to refine their perceptions, to use them for the good of themselves and others? What a different perception they'd have of themselves! Jessica's young friends certainly moved my heart and became my inspiration.

Another beautiful young girl I met was Stephanie, a vivacious four-teen-year-old, who had spent the last eight years in and out of foster care. At seven, her drug-affected mother had tried to kill her. At eight, her mother's boyfriend shot her while attempting to shoot her mother. At nine, she was witness to her older sister, the only remaining person in her life she dearly loved, being killed by a truck. At ten, she was removed from her mother's care and placed with her uncle in another town. That uncle sexually abused her. Then, one of Stephanie's close friends took her own life. Some years later, Stephanie made an attempt on her own life. Thankfully, the rope snapped and her life was spared. Stephanie was now without close family and living in a group home just outside town, awaiting her next foster placement.

One day when Stephanie was visiting for the weekend, she began to share her dream to gain a scholarship to a private school, pursue a higher education and really 'make something of (her) life'. She spoke about her older sister and how painful it was that she'd been accidentally killed so young. Stephanie missed her dearly.

Before long, I experienced that same familiar sensation, the feeling of subtle change in the energy space around us. I knew someone else had entered the space—someone who had a connection to Stephanie. Suddenly, I received a clear image of a skipping rope and asked Stephanie its significance. Stephanie looked back at me in disbelief. 'My sister and I used to play jump rope together when we were little. It was one of our most favourite things,' she replied.

So it was Stephanie's sister in our midst. She was trying to let Stephanie know she'd not gone away, that Stephanie was not alone. What was I to do? This wasn't the time to tune out.

'Now I'm being shown underneath your bed,' I offered. 'It's as if something's under there that no-one else knows about; something special to you.'

'Why are you saying that?' Stephanie replied, her face frozen with shock.

'Well ... I have abilities to see and sense things,' I replied. 'I believe your sister is here, and giving me this information. I feel she knows what's under your bed and she knows how significant that is to you. This is her way of confirming she's here.'

Stephanie looked back at me and her eyes filled with tears: 'No-one else in the whole world knows what I have under my bed. I've never told anyone. I have a special box under there, a small one. That's where I put all my special things. One of the things in that box is my sister's skipping rope, the rope we used to play with when she was alive.'

At that moment another image came into my mind's eye. 'So why would she be showing me a vision of a baseball bat?' I gently asked. It was immediately clear from Stephanie's face that I was referring to a memory that wasn't so warm and fuzzy.

'My sister got angry one day,' she began. 'She was being teased by some local kids who lived in our street. We lived with a foster family there. She picked up a baseball bat and hit one of the kids with it. She hit them hard ... and she ended up going to juvie for it.'

'I see,' I quietly responded, recognising how brutal their lives had been. 'I understand,' I replied, my heart feeling the pain her sister had gone through before she passed over.

It was then I felt drawn to ask her sister in spirit a direct question. 'What have you learnt, Bethany? What have you learnt since you left here?'

At that moment I was given a final powerful message: 'I've learnt a lot. I thought that being violent was being powerful—to hit someone, to see them in pain. I now know that's not power at all. True power comes from the heart.'

All teenagers are unique and special. How I longed to reflect back to them the truth of who they were, and to give them a vision of a world where love was abundant and life was eternal. Even small moments of kindness and compassion in our homes can make a vital difference to vulnerable teens, who long for acceptance and reassuring connection. We can really create a significant cultural shift within our families by moving from disciplining to listening, by empathising rather than criticising. Communicating from a place of transparency of heart, rather than intensity of voice, deepens connection and fosters self-esteem and emotional intelligence. If we want our teenagers to become adults who thrive, we need to reflect their wholeness and completeness, not reflect the need for them to strive to be acceptable or valued only when they attain something or prove their value.

A week later we heard from Mia, Jessica's dear school friend in Australia. Mia phoned Jessica several times that week and communicated a few times with me online. As with Nicole and Stephanie, Mia's journey through her early teens was challenging. She was seeing a counsellor for support, clearly struggling to feel loved, to believe she was of value. Mia asked Jessica if she would be able to visit her in the United States and stay with us for a while, and of course we said she could.

Lauren also entered Jessica's life around this time. She and Jessica quickly became almost inseparable. Like Stephanie, Lauren was playful and gregarious. She had the most beautiful, large, crystal-blue eyes. One day after school, as she and Jessica were watching television and chatting and laughing together, I became suddenly aware of that same energetic shift in the room. A woman appeared in spirit near Lauren. She was about thirty, with long blonde hair. I saw a vision of her singing at a microphone. This time it was a lot easier to share what I was seeing, as Lauren had already told us of her intuition and her acceptance of happenings outside the everyday.

When I asked Lauren who this woman was, she came back without hesitation. 'My mother!' she replied, her face now solemn. 'My mum died when I was very young. She got really sick. She used to sing. I loved listening to her sing.'

At that moment, Jessica suggested they go downstairs to her bedroom to listen to some music, probably to escape my 'weirdness.' They needed some privacy. It was such a delicate balance to allow Jessica's friends their space, while passing on moments that could be valuable for them. As they left, I suddenly heard a song in my mind which I'd heard a number of times on the radio, but I wasn't familiar with the singer or the lyrics. So I went online and did some research, discovering that it was *In My Daughter's Eyes* by Martina McBride, a popular country singer. It became clear that Lauren's mum was asking me to sing it to her, as a message of her unending role as her mum; a clear message that life continues, that love never dies.

Knocking on Jessica's bedroom door, I called out to Lauren: 'Your mum has asked me to sing you something for her. Is it alright if I sing it to you?'

There was a brief pause; then through the closed door Lauren replied: 'Okay!'

The door remained closed. So standing in front of that closed door, I sang the last part of the song as best I could. The words were deeply moving, making reference to how happy she had been as a mother, and while having gone, she was really still there in her daughter's eyes.

Seconds passed in silence, as I finished the song and waited by the door. Suddenly, Lauren opened it and poked her head out. With tears in her gorgeous big, blue eyes, she said: 'My mum loved Martina McBride. She used to sing her songs. She loved country. She used to sing country music.'

I walked back upstairs feeling such fullness in my heart. Once again I had been reassured that when we follow the luminous signs offered by those beyond, learning to move past the discomfort of the left of field moments that often seem awkward or out of place, wonderful outcomes can prevail. Such moments are not only evolutionary opportunities for those here on earth. They are deeply significant opportunities for those dearly departed to pass on long-awaited messages that generate much joy and healing for all.

21

MEETING SHYLO

Within a few days, Jeanie Griggs contacted me. By now it was winter; almost Christmas. Her daughter Shylo, an eighteen-year-old teenager from Northern California, was interested in having some sessions. Jeanie was caring, gentle and supportive. As it turned out, Shylo and her mother were open and interested in the spiritual aspects of life. On learning Shylo's story and the challenges she had faced, I was touched by her courage and resilience.

Shylo had grown up as the youngest and only girl of three children. The family had lived in the picturesque small-town community of Etna in northern California. Shylo's father was a lumberjack, and was addicted to alcohol and drugs. He would often inflict his rage on Shylo's mother, hurting and threatening her and the children. Sometimes Shylo's mother would escape with the children and stay with a close friend, returning when she felt it was safe again.

Such toxic experiences within families have an ongoing destructive impact, as they shatter our self-worth and adversely affect our ability to bond and relate to others in healthy ways. The greater the adverse experiences in childhood, the more significant our chances of suffering ill health and even chronic disease as an adult. All the unspoken emotions remain bottled up inside us, creating unhelpful beliefs about ourselves and the world around us, and limiting our life choices and potential. If we're not able to clear them, these toxic emotional patterns keep on repeating themselves, causing yet another generation to have to deal with painful relationships, financial challenges, health challenges and ongoing crises.

One such occasion that left its mark happened on the morning of Shylo's seventh birthday. Shylo's mother and the three children were enjoying a relaxed morning, helping their mum decorate Shylo's birthday cake. Jeanie had chosen to make an elaborate carousel horse cake. As the horse was placed on top of the cake, Shylo's father stormed into the room, having just woken up. He was down off his drug high of the previous evening, and was mean and extremely angry.

He threatened Shylo's mother, then reached over to a gallon glass jar and threw it on the floor. Shards of glass shattered across the entire kitchen. Jeanie yelled at him to stop, as it was Shylo's birthday, but he just didn't care. Shylo then screamed at him to stop, only to have him grab Shylo by her shoulders, shoving her so hard into the plasterboard wall that the sheeting was indented with Shylo's small frame. The power of the blow terrified her.

Furious at what he had done, Jeanie yelled at Shylo's father and pushed him away. The boys screamed at him too. Taking no notice, he flung open the back door. Then grabbing Shylo's beautiful birthday cake, he threw it out onto the grass just outside the kitchen door and returned to bed.

A short while later, Jeanie drove the children to the safety of her close friend, Carrie, who lived a short distance away. It was there they took refuge from Shylo's father and tried to celebrate Shylo's seventh birthday as best they could.

With the memory of this incident still vivid in Shylo's mind, she spoke of her pain at seeing her mother treated in such a brutal and demeaning way. She was also frustrated with her mother for accepting her fate and remaining with her violent father, saying she would never allow a man to treat her that way.

This feisty girl was riding bareback at the age of three. In time she became a proficient horsewoman, often riding into the mountains, camping up there by the mountain lakes with her rodeo drill team. Fearless and proud, Shylo was outspoken and opinionated, leaving those around her in no doubt about her strongly-held beliefs.

As she rode bareback into those beautiful mountains, Shylo felt a deep, soulful connection to the land. She revered nature, animals and country life. She stood up for what she believed in, never fearing to hold back from saying what she really felt. She was bright at school and her grades were high. She had attended college with strong hopes of continuing her higher education. She wanted to make a real difference in life.

Yet when I first met Shylo she was suffering from the trauma of a head injury, the result of a car accident two years before. I worked with her to assist her to make sense of what had occurred in her life, to empower her to navigate her challenges, so she could move forward with a strengthened version of herself.

After her second session, she emailed me to share her disappointment that she still hadn't been able to access the kind of answers that would alleviate her intense frustration about her car accident. She longed to know exactly why she'd had to go through the car accident, and why she'd had to experience such huge loss as a result. That near fatal car accident had left her with serious brain injuries and subsequent brain changes. She felt different. Her personality had changed. Her forthright nature was left weakened. She felt vulnerable and disempowered, compared to how she'd felt before that fateful day on Salmon Mountain near her hometown of Etna.

The bar was set high for Shylo. Soon I would learn just how high. On a deeper level, Shylo's emotional suffering related to years of trauma, resulting from her father's violence. She was now that vulnerable child all over again. The person she had become was not the person she wanted to be, and had to be. Her strength, competence and resilience had been shattered the day her friend Kelly's car smacked full speed into that huge old tree.

Replying to Shylo's email, I encouraged her to trust the therapeutic process and try to be gentle on herself. I explained that we would work together to see what new insights could be gained in our next session, which she had requested for the following week. Her reply seemed lighter, more hopeful.

Shylo's mother, Jeanie, had taken a call from an old school friend of Shylo's, who said she would stop by the house and drop off a saddle. Shylo became very upset about that arrangement. Since her accident, Shylo had been less tolerant of people visiting. Injury to the pre-frontal part of the brain, like Shylo had, results in compromised brain function. One challenging aspect, common to those with brain injuries like Shylo's, is that those affected can become emotionally dysregulated, meaning they are less capable of monitoring themselves and stopping themselves from getting too emotional. Those affected may display less tolerance and may be more prone to emotional and physical outbursts. Shylo's mother had become her emotional navigator through times where Shylo experienced huge doubt or dismay, or when Shylo was emotionally charged and confronting.

'Let's not do this, Shylo,' said Jeanie gently.

'If you don't understand Mum, no-one will!' And with that, Shylo stormed into her bedroom.

Jeanie began to sweep the kitchen floor, only to have Shylo storm out of her room in a rage. Instinctively, Jeanie raised the broom in defence. Within moments, Shylo walked off down the passage. Jeanie began to sweep the floor again, thinking she would just let things settle for a while before talking with Shylo again.

Seconds later she heard a strange noise, like the dull crack of splitting wood. Thinking Shylo had broken something, she walked down the passage and into Shylo's room, then into her own bedroom. There she found Shylo lying on the floor, barely moving. Shylo had taken her mother's pistol, lay down on the floor and shot herself at point-blank range.

Initially placed on life support at the hospital, Shylo was pronounced dead shortly afterwards. The time of her death was recorded as 2.05pm, the same time she had arrived in the world eighteen years before.

The following day, I received the devastating news of her tragic suicide. That was the day when my life was changed forever.

SHYLO RETURNS

The intensity of Shylo's loss was savage, battering everyone in its wake. Bewildered, my mind endlessly searched for clues as to why she had taken her life. Sitting alone by the bedroom window, I stared out into the nothingness, trying to comprehend what more I could have done. Suddenly, from somewhere behind me, I sensed the energy change. I was about to receive further insight. Eager to communicate with Shylo, I stood up and grabbed a pen and notepad.

Shylo walked into the room with her hair pulled back in a ponytail, her beautiful face so young and soft. Tears flooded my eyes as I wrestled with an avalanche of emotions. I felt incredibly grateful that I could communicate with her from the other side.

'It's strange 'cause they can't hear me,' she began softly. 'So I have to do things to let them know I'm here. With you, it's easy. I just talk with you and you hear me. 'Cause of the link. Heaven cam,' she said, with a lovely smile.

'Is that what it is then?' I said, returning her smile. 'Well, that's why I can sometimes see what you're experiencing. A good thing this heaven cam is, sweetheart. I'm so grateful you can speak to me, and that it's helping you.'

'Kids are coming here all the time. Different kids from all over,' she continued.

'You mean passing over? You mean taking their lives?'

'You have to tell them ... tell them that the choice is final. There's no going back. No waking up and it's all back the way it was. Once you're here, they won't let you go back. You're here and that's it.' Her words were powerful, perceptive.

'They can't get it up here,' she continued, pointing to her head. 'They don't understand what life is. How this all is. I can see now the things you told me about in our sessions, things you could see. Now I can see. And it's amazing. Mum and I used to talk about it. Our ideas of life. But we didn't get close to what it's really like here. You just can't believe it.

'There are people coming and going from here all the time. Decisions ... planning ... amendments ... according to the higher plan for each person. Life here is on lots of different levels. There are different areas, and each area organises and takes care of a specific group. Like a hospital has different wards and buildings, but they're organised in a way that helps people with similar needs.'

Shylo was looking more sporty and fit, and vibrant too. Yet this was not how I knew her to be. Was there going to be anymore she had to share?

Shylo continued: 'Kids have got to hear this message. We have to get this message to them, then they won't do what I did.'

'But what is it we can share Shylo, to really reach them and change them?'

'You!' she said firmly. 'You've really helped me and my mum. They need to know that there is no going back, once they have ended their life. Their life on earth is over. It's finished.'

'But for some people, Shylo, that would be a relief. To kids who feel lost and confused that may seem inviting. To have no more confusion, no more complication, no more overwhelming thoughts or feelings. What can you tell them from where you are, that will make a difference? What is it that you see now, that makes the difference?' I asked.

'From the moment I stepped back away from myself, and saw others coming towards me, I just knew straightaway that I had taken an action (long pause) I had ended something ... and I only realised from being outside of it and looking back at the life I had ... I suddenly realised how special and important and significant that life really was.

'I realised how much my actions, my choices had affected the people who knew me. I saw life moving on without me being a part of it. Without me being able to talk to anybody, to tell them it was a mistake. That I didn't mean what occurred. If I had the opportunity over again ... I would never throw away the choice to remain there.

'You don't realise how special life is, until you get here. Other people come here after being through painful experiences, and they are happy and relieved to be brought here. But young people who choose in a moment to take their life almost always feel their choice ... was not one they would make if they were given a second chance.

'My brother talks to me. Tell him that what he feels when he talks, I hear and feel too. I'm trying to help him understand he hasn't lost me. Tell Mum she looked beautiful today,' she said, with love in her heart for the woman she loved and admired.

This was the day of Shylo's funeral. It was extraordinary to me that Shylo was visiting to communicate about life in spirit.

'Over here we celebrate life,' she continued. 'We realise that being on earth, living and being able to do the things there, is such a privilege. We don't usually see it till we are here—till we have gone. It's like having a vacation then going home and realising how your life was so much more complete while you were away.

'We get taught here. There are others who instruct us, sort of like a coach. They help grow our understanding of things. Everyone wants to be a part of helping those who have recently arrived in spirit to best come to terms with being here. We gather into groups to learn and understand the pathway we've taken, and how to make different choices next time that would take us in a different direction. It also gives us the time to share how we feel about what happened. We listen as others heal. We learn from the wisdom they share with us, as they come to close the memory of their earth life and begin their lives here again.

'After a while, we all feel okay about our new lives here. The first days after leaving earth can be pretty hard to adjust to, because we wished we hadn't taken the steps we did, because we realise the actions we've taken to get here. We often sit here and share with our teachers how different things could have been if we had chosen to continue our lives there on earth instead. That's the game of life. For each person, in every day of their life there where you are, there is so much more opportunity to choose and create the experience you want and the result you want. As we discover how the big picture actually works, we know how to make the best choices. As we learn that life is a great privilege, and that we really do always have choices, we can choose to live. If we had really understood that before we took the actions we did, none of us would be here.'

Shylo paused, then continued: 'My teachers are sharing this with you through me. They send their love and thank for you for what you're doing for us.'

'Thank you!' I whispered, feeling a special warmth in my heart. I paused for a moment, wondering how I could possibly get this message out.

'Just tell them how much we all want them to understand how awesome life is there!' Shylo replied. 'Before you choose a life there, you actually plan where and when and who you will be with. So you choose your family, where in the world you live, and kinda create what time frame you're gonna take to learn the things you need to learn.

'In your recent pathway from Canada to Eastern United States to Ashland where you are now receiving our messages, you actually planned this route in spirit, to give you the experience and ready yourself for your future work. If you chose to pull out of what you had planned, then you would have altered your capacity to learn and become a more elevated soul. You would have denied yourself a great learning experience.'

'What do you do once the phase is over of realising earthly life is precious and that you'd make different decisions if you had another chance?' I asked. 'What do you do then, honey?'

'When we feel we are ready, we can move into a new role. Everything here is through choice. Here we can decide to do different things, based on what learning we feel we most need. Some might choose to be around certain people having life challenges in your world, to be their support person. Others might choose to be around their family members more. They might feel they need to do that, so they can adjust to being here more easily. They might feel they are offering support to their family, and in that way rebalance the pain created by the choices they made in coming here.

'Some might choose to be available to help others who are leaving earth to return here. They may need to give service to someone who has passed over and needs help to come to terms with being back here. If it's someone who hasn't spent too long in your world, then one of us will assist them as a young person to relate to their new life here, to help them feel more comfortable. Sort of like a big brother or sister. Every arrival here is prepared. No matter how many are coming here, no matter their circumstances, everyone is welcome.'

At that moment, I was aware of an older woman joining Shylo in the room and asked: 'So it's really about creating the optimum environment for people to come back to spirit?'

'So many things are happening so fast,' said Shylo. 'I like talking with you. I have so much to say that I want others to hear. People like you are a bridge. We need you to speak for us. We want to make a difference. You have to talk about who you see and what you see. You have to talk to people about life here. It's really important.'

Shylo's insights impacted on me significantly. I made a note to myself to remember to copy the communication directly into my computer, so I didn't lose what she had shared. For a brief moment, I thought I may have to rework a word or two to make it flow better.

Shylo immediately interjected: 'Don't change a word! I like what I said!'

23

OVERCOMING ALL ODDS

It was interesting to see Shylo operate from a new place within herself, now she was living beyond the veil. She certainly seemed to have a distinctly different personality to the girl who came to me for her consultations. She seemed much more assertive, more direct and forthright. I would later learn from her mother, Jeanie, that this was typical of Shylo's previous personality—before her horrific car accident when she was just sixteen.

Her close school friend, Kelly, had been driving the car that fateful day. Kelly had not long had her licence and so was relatively inexperienced. Shylo had been warned only the week before not to ride in the car with Kelly behind the wheel. They had decided to leave Etna High School sometime after 1.20pm, to drive up to Etna Creek on Salmon Mountain, planning to return for Kelly's volleyball practice by midafternoon. Etna Creek was where local teenagers often hung out with friends.

After only a brief visit to Etna Creek, the girls decided to return to school. With their favourite music playing on the CD player at Shylo's feet, the girls were enjoying the music and each other's company. As they emerged from the more densely-forested section of the mountain, onto a flat section of road surrounded by picturesque meadows, they entered the section of roadway locals referred to as Grease Flat.

The car was gathering speed. They approached a bend and, for whatever reason, Kelly took the corner way too fast, losing control. The car ploughed off the road at high speed and smashed head-on into a massive old pine tree several feet off the roadway. It was 2.05pm on that warm September afternoon, the same time Shylo had been born.

The impact happened as Shylo leant forward to change the CD player, and the front left side of Shylo's head took the full brunt of the collision. Her skull was fractured and her brain traumatised, leaving Shylo with a severe brain injury. Both girls sat slumped and unconscious, trapped in the car crushed against the tree. And both were critically injured.

Shylo's Aunt Margaret had arrived at the school earlier that day, to pick up her older daughter Amber. She chatted briefly with Shylo and Kelly, then left with Amber, heading first to the grocery store, then to collect the mail and fuel the car. With her daughter Amber, her younger daughter Boston and a friend visiting for the weekend, they drove out of town and entered Grease Flat at the base of Salmon Mountain. Loaded up with supplies and their pets, they were heading for their weekend home on the other side of Salmon Mountain. The scenic journey would take them a little over two hours across the forested mountain, then a relaxing weekend awaited them.

When Margaret entered Grease Flat, it was only minutes after the crash. Little did she realise she was about to experience one of the most challenging moments she would have to ever face. They stopped at the scene, hoping to help the driver and passenger trapped inside.

Having completed Emergency Medical Technician training some months before, Margaret climbed out of her car and walked over towards the wreck. Amber stayed by her mother's side. As they approached the massive pine tree, the crumpled wreck sat eerily still. They were confronted by what they saw. Both driver and passenger were slumped forward and appeared unconscious. There was no sound. It seemed like time had stopped.

Doubting she could do anything at all, Margaret felt immobilised by the tragedy. What could she do? She needed help. A man who had also been driving past was already trying to help the female driver of the car.

Margaret and Amber moved to the passenger side of the vehicle. As they moved closer, Amber recognised Shylo's black hair clip. She and her mother stood motionless with shock. How could this be Shylo? Amber and Margaret had just seen her at school, less than half an hour before. The girls must have left school only minutes after and driven past them, when they stopped for food and fuel.

At that painful moment, only one thing mattered above all else: to save Shylo's life, to prevent her from dying.

Margaret gently reached through the open window of the passenger door and felt for Shylo's pulse. It was faint. She knew straightaway that Shylo's injuries were critical. Her head was hanging forward, and Margaret realised Shylo was unable to breathe properly. Her airway was obstructed. She was choking on her seat belt. As Margaret slowly lifted Shylo's head, she noticed the horrific gash above her left eye. Blood was already pooling in her lap. Her immediate concern was that Shylo was going to bleed to death.

Turning back to Amber, she told her to hurry back to the car and fetch her EMT bag and oxygen. Within moments, Amber was back. The bag was on the ground, open and ready. Amber passed her mother the mask and oxygen, and Margaret fitted the mask to Shylo's face to help her breathe.

Hearing a sudden voice behind her, Margaret looked around to see a woman standing hesitantly next to the car. She was a resident of the house closest to the wreck. The force of the car ploughing at high speed into the huge pine tree had been so severe that several pictures hanging on the wall in her home had crashed to the ground. Margaret instructed the woman to call 911 then confirm that paramedics were on their way.

At that moment, Kelly began to regain consciousness. Aware of their terrifying predicament and her chronic pain, she began to scream and struggle to free herself from the wreckage. Concerned, Margaret called out to the man on Kelly's side of the car: 'Try to keep her still! Try not to move her! Don't let her move!'

Relief came moments later when the paramedics finally arrived. Seeing Margaret already attending to Shylo, they made the decision to treat Kelly first. With one eyelid almost severed and hanging down over her cheek, a broken pelvis and a broken arm, Kelly had sustained significant injuries. The paramedics were yet to realise that Shylo was the more critically injured of the two.

Continuing to work on Shylo, Margaret applied pressure to Shylo's bleeding head wound, then called for Amber to phone Shylo's mother to get there fast. Shylo was still unconscious and unresponsive. The female paramedic came to assist Margaret strap the collar on Shylo's neck. Margaret gently held her through the open window, as the door was still jammed shut. She was scared that if Shylo didn't receive medical help soon, her life could be lost.

The decision was made to use a crowbar to try to open the passenger door and free Shylo from the wreck. Numbed by shock, Margaret didn't realise until days later that she had actually been injured during the attempt to force open the door. All the while Margaret stood against the car door, her arms through the open window, holding Shylo's head up so she could breathe, as the paramedics made several unsuccessful attempts to prise open the jammed door.

Eventually, they managed to slide Shylo's unconscious body out the back of the vehicle and into the waiting ambulance. Kelly was already inside on a gurney. By this stage, Shylo's mother was entering Grease Flat. The ambulance slowed down to allow the paramedic to explain the urgency of getting the girls to hospital. A decision was made en route, by the paramedics and medical staff on standby at the local hospital, to airlift Shylo to Medford Hospital just over the border in Oregon, where a neurosurgical team was on standby.

The helicopter sat on the airfield, as they prepared Shylo for the flight. Jeanie and Shylo's Aunt Margaret were now at Shylo's side. Suddenly, Shylo went into a seizure. Desperately scared that her beautiful daughter was about to die, Jeanie cried out: 'Can't you get her into that helicopter any faster?' The paramedics explained they needed to stabilise Shylo before she could be flown out. So Jeanie remained close, willing her daughter to live, as she watched each breath Shylo took under the oxygen mask.

The rotor blades of the helicopter finally began to whir into action, and Shylo was on her way to the Trauma Unit at Providence Medford Medical Centre. After three hours of lifesaving neurosurgery, Shylo lay in a coma on life support in the critical care unit, battling for her life. Shylo's family stood vigil with her, day after day, praying she would soon regain consciousness.

After three harrowing weeks in a coma, Shylo finally opened her eyes. The extent of her injuries and the recovery she faced were significant. Shylo had to learn to swallow again, to correctly sequence her words, to problem solve and gradually achieve more complex tasks. She was to face another gruelling four weeks in hospital, receiving continuing medical treatment and daily inpatient rehabilitation.

One day Shylo lay in her hospital bed, staring up into the corner of the ceiling above her. Looking across at her daughter and noticing her fixed intense stare, Jeanie asked: 'Shylo, what is it you're looking at up there?'

'Comet and Venus,' replied Shylo, her gaze still fixed on the ceiling above. 'And this is a lesson for you all!'

At that moment, Jeanie felt a strange knowing pass through her. Then she slowly sat back down next to Shylo and gently took her hand, wondering if Shylo was perhaps tapping into some higher force in and around her.

Shylo had a further four months in outpatient rehabilitation, learning to stand and walk again. To repair and retrain her brain after such substantial injuries became a long and tedious task. Another hurdle was coping with the reactions of her friends to the changes in her personality and emotions. That vivacious, confident, feisty friend they once knew and loved was now subdued.

It was during Shylo's recovery that she began to seek deeper answers to life's significant questions. Louise Hay's book, *You Can Heal Your Life*, began Shylo's personal journey of discovery, leading her to discover a greater depth and meaning in herself and her life. Her mother felt she had 'matured beyond her years.' Shylo's quest was to understand the higher reason for her accident and her life challenges. This became her passion. It was this same quest that eventually led Shylo to me.

The work we had begun in her consultations with me offered Shylo a level of insight regarding her spiritual purpose, the spiritual growth that would be achieved through her participation in the accident, and her challenges following it.

Hearing about her accident, I was given profound insights into the time Shylo was in her coma. Shylo seemed to be communicating with 'others' beyond this third-dimensional world. These others seemed to be supporting her, reminding Shylo what she needed to learn through this experience. Having to face the unfolding challenges of awakening from her coma, being more dependent and feeling weaker and less capable, was a great challenge for her. Shylo was clearly resistant to this new reality, though it wasn't without meaning for her. She came to understand there was a higher purpose: that real learning was to be gained through her accident and beyond it. This was the means by which she could attain and complete certain lessons required for her soul growth.

As for many of us, this learning wasn't easy for Shylo. We want to be wiser, but we don't necessarily want the challenges that are sometimes needed to get us to that place of higher understanding and higher elevation. Like it or not, she would have to work through the loss of no longer being the young woman she had previously been. Her personality changes following the accident were marked. They left her feeling her spark had been taken from her. She remarked to me during her sessions: 'I used to be vivacious, but now I'm different. I liked being the way I was.'

At that moment, I had little understanding of how marked the changes were for Shylo. But after Shylo took her own life and moved beyond her earthly existence, our positions significantly shifted. I was now the reluctant student, and she the teacher. As I came to know Shylo's forthright personality more fully, it was clear to me this was the way it was meant to be.

24

TRAVELLING
BETWEEN WORLDS

The warm spring night seemed particularly still. Jessica had gone to bed early. I always adored the sacredness of night. After cleaning up, I suddenly sensed Shylo was about to visit. Sitting at my computer, I waited until I began to feel a strange sensation of dizziness. Seconds passed. I became aware I was losing anchor in my current location. I was being slowly transported to the moment of Shylo's car accident.

Already she was slumped and unconscious. Somehow I could see, sense and hear what was happening at the accident site, and what was simultaneously occurring around Shylo in the spirit realm. Next, I watched a tunnel of swirling energy open up above the car wreck, a sort of portal between dimensions. People in spirit were looking down through the tunnel to the scene below, commenting: 'How does she look? She's not supposed to die here. She's important. She carries a message. Does she look all right? Feel her pulse!'

At that moment, my perspective changed. I was now able to see a doctor in spirit crouched down next to the passenger car door. He was holding Shylo's wrist through the door, as if the door was there yet not there. From both the style of his clothing and a sudden knowing, I became aware he had been a doctor in the 1970s. I sensed he had lived and practised in the greater San Francisco area. He held Shylo's wrist, while looking intently at his watch.

Then he stood up, his hands in his pockets with an obvious look of concern. I heard him tell the others beyond the tunnel: 'She's okay.' But the inflection in his voice suggested a deeper concern, as he added: 'She'll be okay. She's strong. It's tough for her though. She knew that. She wanted to do this, to go through all of this. She knew it would be hard. She knew it would be painful. It's not the end though. This is not the end for her here.'

The depth of empathy in his voice struck me. It was a privilege to be shown this review of the accident from another perspective. While Shylo was to make it through the crash alive, the doctor showed a great deal of empathy for what she had taken on in this paralysing moment in her human and soul's journey. Life was not going to be easy for Shylo.

He was still concerned about how she would pull through, even though this event was 'supposed' to occur. It was touching for me to see him recall how painful life can be here on this earth plane. He was also remembering how his own patients would often not make it. I sensed this was all part of his learning and request for learning—to be here at this point of Shylo's accident, to support her at this moment. Perhaps this was to prepare for his own return to earth?

I felt a car pull up and sensed this was Shylo's Aunt Margaret. Some moments passed. The scene then morphed to the moment when the ambulance had arrived. Stretchers stood near the car. I could see Kelly being taken out earlier than Shylo. Paramedics were working on Shylo as the scene played out.

As I sat with my arms resting on my desk, staring into the scene unfolding beyond my computer screen, I was struck to see how close to death Shylo had been. It was like a centimetre closer and she would have passed. It was as if death itself was standing waiting for her over near the trees, somehow holding the entire scene in its grasp. One of the paramedics held an intravenous drip and bag above Shylo. There was a tangible feeling of tension. Everyone was clearly affected by the traumatic nature of the injuries sustained, watching each passing second, as if to hold onto Shylo's life for one more moment.

At that point in the 'film sequence,' I stopped and spoke out loud: 'Shylo, why are you showing me this?'

Suddenly, a more official man appeared from the realm of spirit. Clearing his throat he said: 'This is not a replay you are seeing. This is the actual event. Time is not sequential as it is often experienced on earth. Time is simply a device through which we can manifest the intricacies of experience. This is done by altering thought, sound and matter. Time can extend or contract through thought transference. This is not difficult for those who are adept at altering matter, perception and frequency. Time in itself is not linear.'

Stunned by these revelations, I sat at my desk waiting further information. Things had become silent again. It was now 11.55pm. Then without warning, my body suddenly felt like it had lost energy and I slumped forward. My awareness was shifting. It was being taken once again to the time of the accident.

The paramedics were monitoring Shylo's heart, because of the level of trauma her body and brain had sustained. The scene felt tense. Then I suddenly heard Shylo's voice from somewhere behind me. She too seemed to be observing her predicament: 'I'm alright, really!' she assured me.

By now we were inside the ambulance, and Shylo was in spirit next to me. She was sitting up in the ambulance, behind her body on the stretcher. At first glance, the ambulance appeared 'normal.' Then, it appeared to have one entire side missing, so we could see through it.

I then noticed that the space surrounding the ambulance was the void of space-time. Initially, I wondered why that might be. It seemed grey in colour, but was swirling, moving and even conscious. It seemed we were nowhere in particular, sort of suspended. Then I wondered if we were being transported into some type of time tunnel or section of space-time.

At the same time, I began to realise that I was able to change my viewing perspective at will. At one moment, I would be observing the ambulance from the outside, from the space-time void. Then, my viewpoint would be from inside, where everything looked and seemed like a 'normal' ambulance.

My body suddenly felt an energy slump again, as I was connected more fully with Shylo's unconscious body. There was an increasing sensation on my forehead. I became aware she had been given drugs to ease the pain. Then everything seemed strange and slowed down as if time, as we know it, had been altered.

The very next thing I became aware of, as I looked from outside into the ambulance where Shylo was lying on the stretcher, was an immediate sense of intense, brilliant, bright light. Then suddenly the scene morphed once more. The ambulance now sat to my left on what appeared to be a highly-polished floor. It had been transported there—somehow. Without warning, the phrase 'by way of molecular regeneration' slipped into my mind, immediately answering my query as to how the ambulance had got here.

The ambulance was motionless, parked in this special room. Its highly-polished floor was somehow familiar to me. It was as if I had been there before sometime in my soul's experience. The room had an otherworldly feel to it. As soon as I observed this more information flooded my mind, explaining the otherworldly aspect of this place. Astonishingly, this room could alter itself, to be seen or not. There was a very different light and feeling to it—subdued but with a distinctive feeling of intelligence within the light. The way learning took place here was by instant downloads.

There wasn't anyone in the rear of the ambulance now. The doors were wide open. The drivers were slumped down in the front section of the vehicle. They looked to be asleep, which felt decidedly eerie. It was as if they had been placed in an alternative state of consciousness, while this intervention was taking place. It was disturbing to look at them in this suspended state, so I quickly looked away.

My awareness was suddenly drawn to the far right of this special room. The radiant and yet soft light entranced me. It had its own consciousness. It was strangely familiar too. Shylo lay unconscious on a table; just like a medical examination table. Yet, as I studied the table, I instantly understood it to be a monitoring device, as if it too had an intelligence and was able to align with what needed to be achieved for Shylo, at the highest level of her being.

There was a group of 'others' surrounding Shylo's body, bathed in the light. Some seemed to be medical doctors, while others seemed like luminous beings of light. Perhaps they were angels. There was much activity around Shylo. I sensed the speed and precision of those working on her. This intervention was supporting Shylo to ensure the outcome was in alignment with the ultimate plan for Shylo's own learning, and, through her, greater learning for others.

As I looked at the table Shylo was lying on with everyone around her, there was so much light. It was so extraordinarily bright, I could hardly see her. Yet somehow, I could also see Shylo clearly. As I watched her lying on this special table, I suddenly realised that her face, her forehead, appeared undamaged. There was no injury at all. As quickly as my mind noticed this, I received further understanding.

In this special environment, there was no requirement for the injury to be present in her body at all. The 'others' assisting her enabled Shylo to be held outside her experience of being traumatised by the accident, and at the same time aligned Shylo's cellular awareness to the experience of being healed. This is how these beings were able to assist her. By holding Shylo in a state of optimum wellness, the consciousness of the cells in her physical body was then able to align with a state of health and healing, rather than trauma.

The light was an altered energy environment, a unified field of frequency. The doctors and others in spirit assisting Shylo worked within this special high-frequency environment of unconditional love. Within this unified field of love was an absolute unwavering, unconditional intention that there would be a higher outcome for Shylo as a result of her accident. This field of higher love and intention sustained her at that quantum level as she healed, overriding any trauma she had previously experienced. This enabled Shylo's cellular consciousness, and thus her physical cellular body, to resonate with a state of health, rather than trauma. So, as I gazed towards the table, I saw Shylo suspended in a state of absolute health and healing.

The length of time needed for the 'others' to enter our earth-based time frame, seize the ambulance and somehow transport it into their dimension of space-time, occurred in a split second of our earth-time— even less. However, I was shown that from this realm's experience, the length of time actually taken for this remarkable intervention to play out was much longer, even though it only measured probably one nanosecond of our earth time.

Seizing the ambulance with Shylo in it seemed necessary to prevent her from dying, before she was able to receive the necessary emergency medical treatment at the hospital in Oregon. In this way, Shylo's injuries were 'altered', allowing her a safer passage forward in her soul's journey, so that the next phase of her life script here on earth could be realised.

Being allowed to witness these events unfolding was astounding, deeply humbling. I sat motionless at my desk. Suddenly my hands left the keyboard, and moved swiftly around in the air in front of me. Some energy work was being carried out just in front of my head. After several moments, my hands expanded and my arms opened out. I noticed a distinct shift in time and place. Within seconds, I felt my awareness shift out of Shylo's place of higher healing to an earthly location.

I received a clear vision of Shylo's mother, Jeanie, attending to a horse. She seemed to be brushing it. Perhaps this was Shylo's horse. I heard her talking to Shylo as she groomed the horse, recalling times when she and Shylo had groomed the horse together, when Shylo would ride or perform special moves with her rodeo drill team.

It was now 12.15am and I was feeling increasingly tired. This was often the case when I was brought back from operating at a much higher level of heightened awareness than in normal daily life. However, as this sudden lethargy entered my mind, I clearly heard Shylo say: 'Write this down please!'

'Okay Shylo,' I immediately replied.

A cool chill swept over me. There was a distinctly different tone to our interaction now. Something was about to be shared of a more personal nature. Perhaps that was why I had 'received' the vision about Shylo's mother, who I knew was in the depths of grief and loss. I took a deep breath, stretched my head and neck a little, and then sat patiently awaiting the communication. As I listened, I was struck by the power and emotion of Shylo's words. It was only then I realised Shylo was speaking about the moment she ended her life.

We'd moved on from the car accident she'd survived and the months of rehabilitation. The moment Shylo was now sharing was the moment just after she had passed over. 'I wanted to stop it, when I realised what I'd done. I was hurting; I knew that. At first there were moments, just moments, when I wondered what was happening. Mum came in and saw me, and sat on the floor and held me.'

At that moment I began to sob uncontrollably. Some moments passed, then summoning what strength remained, I regained enough composure to continue to write down what Shylo was telling me.

'It's impossible to say exactly which moment I realised what I'd done,' Shylo continued. 'But it wasn't long after that I felt I wasn't alone. It felt serious. I felt others close to me, but far enough away that they didn't disturb me. It didn't seem like a surprise they were there. They seemed to allow me to slowly realise that I was slipping out of that moment of being with Mum. My energy was moving away from that experience. I was beginning to feel like I was looking at it, rather than being actually there and feeling it.

'As the moments passed, my life on earth became more and more distant. The area surrounding me was closing up. It was the sensation of being drawn into a different space, beyond where I lay with my mum holding me. It was a place not far away. It was like looking through a round picture window. Like you think the window's not there, then slowly you realise the window separates you from what is really there. At that point, those people were standing behind me. Not close. But I knew they were there ... My feeling of them became stronger as I seemed to leave that old world—that place where I used to be, and where I was no longer able to be. I didn't know it then, but I was coming back to creation. I felt a bit dizzy, kind of light-headed ... and then I began to hear noise, like whisperings, sensations of sound. Not spoken by someone, but in my head.'

As Shylo spoke, I was there in the experience with her, and could see and sense what she was seeing and sensing. It was then I clearly heard another female voice. It was soft and understanding. She talked about Shylo to the others who stood alongside her saying: 'She is almost ready now.'

At that moment I was suddenly frozen within the intensity of what she was saying and what it meant: that Shylo was almost at the point of realising she had truly ended her life, that she was no longer 'alive.' In that one brief moment, that one pull of the trigger, Shylo had ended her precious life.

Once again, I was filled with the depth of this tragedy—of Shylo's actions and the consequences of those actions. The experience was so intense, I suddenly wondered if I was still breathing. When I checked I was, but only just. I sat motionless, so deeply confronted by what I had witnessed.

If there had been one moment before she pulled the trigger that could have been changed, the outcome would have been so different for Shylo. She would have been able to go on living her beautiful life, immersed in the lives of her family, friends and community. It was like a pebble thrown into a large pond. All the ripples irrevocably changed everything in their path. In that one moment, Shylo's life here on this earth plane had gone.

I sat at my computer feeling the devastation of what had happened. Reaching up and slowly removing my glasses, I threw them down on the papers and journals piled next to my computer, feeling utterly powerless. My eyes filled with tears.

Within seconds though, I was fully back at the scene of Shylo's passing over, seeing and sensing the two women and a man who were walking with Shylo now, escorting her away from her initial location in spirit. They were talking with her about what was happening. As they walked, I noticed the energy environment behind them was changing. Nothing seemed solid. They were creating their surroundings by their intentions. Initially, there appeared to be a corridor or passageway; but once they had walked Shylo through each section of this corridor, it once again became formless. It looked to me as if they were actually travelling in time and space, that they had created the 'corridor' as something familiar and comforting for Shylo, something she could relate to in this early phase of her arrival in spirit. As she moved through the realms of spirit, they seemed to be taking her to a place deeper in time itself.

As I took in the unfolding spectacle in front of me, a higher explanation for it was suddenly made clear. I was told that: 'It's very simply an energy space utilised for receiving souls who are passing over from earthly life, a portal into the heart of creation. This was a 'fluid' space, that was created to ensure the optimum environment for the soul's passage from earth to the world of spirit and then on through, deeper into space and time where he or she would then live, until they chose to return to earth.'

Shylo's interactions were providing me with a far greater understanding of the afterlife, which in turn brought so much more meaning to my everyday life. Shylo was now the teacher. The more I let go of the struggle and emotional suffering around her passing, the easier it became for her to communicate with me. Our latest interactions enabled me to glimpse what a feisty, forthright girl she had once been, before we first met. Her contact with me was life-changing. I was now living in-between worlds.

I would never know when my next interaction with Shylo might be. Sometimes it would be late at night, at other times during the day. What was clear was that the veil between worlds was thinning.

25

MOMENTS OF DOUBT

My life was expanding to accommodate Shylo's frequent visits, which soon became a regular part of life. It was during an everyday moment with Shylo's mother, Jeanie, that I noticed the energy environment of the room unexpectedly shift. Shylo suddenly entered the space. She was standing in spirit just to my right.

Her mother had come to visit me and had just been tearfully expressing how much she missed Shylo. She spoke of how very close they had been. Shylo appeared, carrying a basketball. With her was an older man, wearing a trucker's hat. I described him to Jeanie as having been involved with car repairs. Jeanie immediately said this man was Jeanie's stepfather, someone Shylo was fond of. He had died only a few months before Shylo herself had passed.

In a moving interaction, Shylo told her mother it was now time to stand in her personal power and that, like the game of basketball, she must play her moves with determination and precision. At that point Jeanie sat forward on the sofa, explaining that basketball was one of Shylo's favourite sports as a teenager. From Shylo's forthright uncompromising manner, Jeanie now felt she was encouraging her mother, just as she used to do when living at home. Experiencing Shylo's feistiness brought Jeanie such warmth and healing, along with many tears.

Towards the end of our visit, I walked downstairs to collect something from my bedroom for Jeanie. I was surprised to see a basketball sitting in the middle of the downstairs landing. Jessica didn't play basketball. She didn't even own a basketball. Where had it come from? At that moment, Jessica opened her bedroom door. When I asked her where the basketball had come from, she said she'd found it in the grass and felt moved to pick it up and bring it home.

I picked up the well-loved orange basketball, which looked just like the one Shylo was holding in spirit, and joyfully presented it to Shylo's mother, telling her how it came to be in our home. 'Here. This is for you!' I said, my face radiant. 'Shylo clearly intended this as a message to you. It's the first time a basketball has ever been in my house!'

Within a week, Shylo returned to visit. I had been sitting writing for some hours, when an unexpected change occurred in the energy surrounding me. I looked up to see Shylo walk in and seat herself on the chair next to my desk. 'I appreciate you!' Shylo said, as she sat down.

'Thank you, Shylo. I appreciate you too,' I replied, my heart radiant with love for her.

'My mother sent you those things because I asked her to,' she continued, referring to the audio tapes on my desk.

Shylo's mother had a strong feeling she needed to send the tapes to me. They were copies of the recordings of my conversations with Shylo's mother, when Shylo had shown up with the basketball and had given her mother some meaningful advice. Clearly, Shylo was assisting her mother and me with this project between worlds.

'I want you to tell her thanks. She's dedicated. I like that about her,' Shylo continued, now clearly gutsier than I had previously known her to be. 'You've seriously just gotta forget about all this other stuff and focus on what you've gotta do,' she said, referring to my recent preoccupation with clients and my usual day-to-day duties as a mum. She was also referring to my moments of doubt, wondering where all this unexpected journey was taking me—doubts which had led to me to avoid my writing.

'I want to tell you something,' she said, softening a little. 'You have made it better for me to be here, okay? So you've just got to keep trusting this is moving towards something bigger. When you doubt, it's a trap! It's all a trap! There are so many bigger things to get to and to be concerned about. I know. I've seen what's out there. I know we've got a lot to do!'

'Okay, Shylo. I will just have to stop doubting what I am doing and surrender.'

'Being here gives me access to other things, other places,' Shylo continued. 'It's like I'm in service. It's a way of serving. It's easier now that you feel better about me being here. I like it better when you're not hurting so much,' she said, her caring bringing tears to my eyes.

'I like it better when I'm not hurting so much too,' I replied smiling.

'Focus and be determined! Just write and focus!'

She went to walk off, then suddenly stopped and looked back towards me saying: 'Go to bed. I will talk to you later. You go to bed!' Then she was gone. I relented and retired to bed.

Several days later, the same sudden shift in the energy around me occurred again. I was enjoying some easy listening music. A photo of our special friend, Professor John Mack, with his arms around Jessica and me sat proudly on our mantelpiece. It had been taken during his recent visit and I had framed it that afternoon. I missed John so much now we were on the west coast. My mind also held thoughts of Shylo.

I was about to begin writing about Shylo's interactions and insights from the place she referred to as 'creation,' when suddenly a powerful loving light pervaded the room. I sat back, taking in its splendour. The entire space was bathed in a beautiful sacred light presence, exquisite and completely loving. Somewhere in my heart I knew this place, this light, spoke to me of my true soul home.

At that moment I saw Shylo's face, so I moved over to my desk, sat down in front of my computer, closed my eyes and took a deep breath.

Within moments, Shylo began to talk: 'Along the way, everything gets easier. You begin to accept being here in spirit. People are kind,' she explained. 'It's not like where you are. Generally, people stay here in spirit until they have come to a new understanding of themselves and their pathway. This is a place of learning. We are not here just to be somewhere. It has purpose. We celebrate life here. It's easy. Life is easy here. If you want something, or you want to experience something, you have it. You can have an experience to bring you closer to a better understanding of what you are supposed to learn.

'So here you occupy your time with growth. We learn. It's a big school. Everybody learns. We like to learn. It's simple. Once we acknowledge what we need to do, then we can attend to it. You don't feel like it's a chore or that you don't want to do it. You know it will help you to overcome something, or feel better about something. Learning here is like sitting down and having a cup of coffee with someone. Just sitting and listening and being friends. It's a place of caring. It helps you know your goals and what you love to do. Everything we do, we get help with. No-one's alone here. Everyone has other people to help them. There are never people who have no-one to help them.

'There is a strong sense of community. It's because of the connection; we are all connected. No-one has anything to hide here. There's no point. Just like I used to say to my mum: just go do it! Don't be afraid. It doesn't matter what people think of you. Who cares what people will think? Their opinion doesn't matter. Don't restrict yourself because you're thinking: *What will other people think if I take that action?* It doesn't matter. All that matters is that you do what you feel is right inside your heart.'

At that moment I was drawn back to the feeling of loving light around me. I remarked how radiant and beautiful the space had become. Then I noticed a tingling sensation around the periphery of my body. Closing my eyes again, I saw Shylo and smiled at her effortlessly. I felt such love for her I struggled to hold back my tears.

Moments later, my emotions began to settle and Shylo continued: 'Nothing is worth dying for. Not showing anyone anything, not proving anything to anyone, not attempting to escape out of a feeling that you just can't seem to run from. It creates a lot of pain for the people you love. You can't believe what they go through. Nothing can prepare you for that. I try to talk with my mum. Sometimes she feels I'm there. I know she listens to me. I always know that. She tries really hard.'

Again I was fighting back my tears. 'I love you Shylo, with all my heart!' I said, as tears flowed down my cheeks. 'I know me crying like this isn't really helpful to the process,' I added. Then, finding my emotional balance, I insisted we keep going with our work.

Slowly, Shylo's communication resumed. 'Attempts to make contact from here are really hard. You don't want the people you love to feel the pain. You want to try to fix their suffering. You want to say something funny to make them laugh. But they can't hear you anymore. You remember a time when you did make them laugh, and it settles you a little to recall that memory. Then you come to a different place. You see you can't fix things, so you just sit with them to give them comfort. It's a peaceful feeling you can transfer to them. We learn that here, because we know most people can't hear us.

'We have friends here and that helps. We do things together. We make plans to accomplish things we would like to have happen. On a group level, we can be more powerful and affect things more. We get together in groups with other people who have a similar goal, or something they want to experience or do,' Shylo explained. 'In that way, we can share the learning and make a bigger impact. Like in an earthquake, where there are lots of people in distress. We work together to help calm them. Well, we try. We move in and around people in pain or distress. It helps us to learn about what people go through.

'These experiences bring people new insights about themselves or others, or life in general. It's all to do with growing—it's always about growing. We don't just do this to feel the pain. We do this to grow through feeling the pain. So when we hold a person in that painful place, we can join with them and create a barrier of strength to help them survive their experience. Then when they recover, they can offer learning to others by relating their experience.

'We can choose to offer to support a person in this way, or sometimes we're asked to participate in group learning, to bring us all to a new level of awareness. At other times, we participate in events so others can grow. We assist other people to learn. So we might be called in to help with people who are experiencing something in your dimension, or in other dimensions, other places, other times. It's more complicated than you think.'

At this point in the communication, Shylo paused. I sensed she was about to share more personal information, closer to her heart. So I remained at my desk. Then suddenly, I felt a wave of cool chills over my shoulders and across my neck, as I saw an image of Shylo's mother. 'Mum never did anything to hurt me,' Shylo reflected. 'All she ever did was to help support me.'

This was all very emotional, and important information too. I began to feel concerned I wasn't hearing Shylo correctly. My emotions were affecting my ability to hear her, so I asked Shylo to help me. Suddenly, my hands lifted off the keyboard and turned towards me. I felt a flutter of energy through my body. I knew Shylo was assisting me, and immediately the clarity was restored.

'There is so much to do over here. Always choices about what direction you want to go in, what group you want to be involved with. It's kind of like summer camp. Sometimes we are prepared for events that will bring a number of people across, events you would call a disaster. It's really an opportunity for those people to leave their physical life. Then others around them grow, as a result of their departure.

'Every experience is about growth. As someone you love leaves their life there, it is always a message not to waste the life you have. Don't let any event pass without stopping and asking yourself: *How is my life different from this experience? How can I learn from it, or become something other than what I have been?* It's really important to experience these events as learning moments. That's where the real point of life hits home. You can really see the value of what's real.

'One of the things we often hear from people, when they start the first part of their learning on arriving here, is that they wish they could have engaged in their life more—done more of what they really wanted to do. But changing the way you live your life is not easy for many people. I see that more clearly now I'm here. When I was where you are, I used to get frustrated with people doing things that didn't make any sense. I really wanted people to take notice of what I thought, and what they were doing that sometimes annoyed me. I would get so frustrated when it wasn't clear to other people, the way it was clear to me.

'It's like some people live their life in a daydream. They don't think about their actions, how many people will be affected by what they do and don't do. Some people don't want to get involved. They want to leave it to others to make the changes.

'Well, the world needs everybody to take action, to step up and do what needs to be done. Everybody can make the changes. Everybody. Even kids. People seem to have forgotten the value of simple things, more than things that cost a lot. They don't matter. It's sharing time together that matters—laughing, having fun, enjoying those special moments with the people you care about. Those moments are what we think about most when we get here. We never even think about the things we had. There's no value in things. It's the people you care about, the times they made you laugh and made you feel really strong, proud and happy. The times you gave it your best, then came through and gained a sense of confidence ... this is what really matters most.

'I don't blame anyone for me being here. I never felt that way. I had to accept that's what I did. I just didn't want to think anymore. But if I had just walked out of there instead of reaching for Mum's gun, then that moment would have passed, and we could have just ... I could have had the life I had come to live. It wasn't like I wanted to leave. I just wanted to stop the thoughts about how different I was from before the car wreck. I felt different. Changed. It was hard to understand that I couldn't just get better.

'It was something I never accepted and it caused me to feel like sometimes I didn't want to try. I think that if I had just been able to let go of wanting to be the same as I used to be, I could have accepted that who I'd become after the accident was alright too. I know a lot of people loved me and wanted me to know that who I was then was enough. I know that. Lots of people felt like that. But I just had expectations for myself and ... it was like a hurdle that I just couldn't seem to get over.

'When someone dies the way I did, they lose a turn. You can't just decide to come back. I've seen so many times when people die and they want to go back, they can't. You have to wait until you know what caused you to leave the life you had. You have to wait until things have changed for you, to have an opportunity to come back. Sometimes that's tough on people, once they come to understand how things really have to be.

'Most people who leave the way I did don't mean to be here. They come here and just want to take it all back. They look at all the people they left behind, who have to go through so much pain and feel so sad. The pain caused by dying the way I did doesn't stop when you're gone. It just keeps going, like a long rope. It just doesn't stop hurting for the people you left behind.

'It's not an intelligent choice. It's not even powerful. It's just that people don't see that you can make other decisions. You can find a way to feel free from the pain. I didn't make that decision. The decision I made led to my leaving a life that I really appreciated. I love my mum. I never wanted to blame her. But what I did left her feeling like she had done something wrong. I never felt she did anything wrong. She was the best mum. She worked hard and she never did much for herself. She loved us kids and she wanted us to have a great life. If I could have stopped anything, I would have stopped the pain she went through after I shot myself. I didn't think that I would die. I didn't know what it meant. I just knew I had to do something that would end the pain and the thoughts about not being enough, not being the same as before.

'When I looked back in at my mum in so much pain, I knew I had done something I couldn't take back. I couldn't decide in that moment that I had made the wrong decision and just step back into my life. It was finished and I couldn't go back. I couldn't ride anymore, be with my friends or laugh and have fun, or do anything that I loved there. It was my decision. I knew that, but it wasn't a choice that I could change. There wasn't a second chance. I left, and I couldn't go back.

'I am here and now I have to wait until I learn what I need to learn; then the moment of understanding will come. Returning to earth will then be the most important way of contributing and understanding my life more. I wasn't given that chance. It stopped once I pulled the trigger. If I could, I wouldn't have done it. It makes everything harder. It's not easy to watch the people you care about go through such big changes inside and in their own life. It's so hard to see what your decision did to everyone.

'There are so many other ways to be heard, to make things less painful. It's so easy to see that once you are here—once they show you all the moments where things could have been different. Even in a thought. Just one thought makes so much difference. I wish I'd have made the choice to make my life continue on. That would've been so great. I would've done lots more things, and had lots more time with my family and my friends; made more friends and done more things. But I can't, 'cause I'm here. Now I have to wait till the time is open for me to return.

'Elizabeth, I love what you do. I love the difference you make to people's lives. It's the best thing. I've noticed how you show people who come to you how to think, how to choose ways to make them grow and feel better about who they are. It's really important, because you make them see their lives are valuable. That's really special.' Then Shylo added: 'I'm leaving again now. I'm ready to go back.'

Shylo stood up from the chair I was sitting on, then turned around and stood behind me. It was as if she and I had been merged, to enable the clear flow of information from her to me. She was dressed in a black summer top with small shoulder straps. Her hair was in a ponytail. She wore casual blue jeans.

Shylo waited for me to complete writing. Then I saw her look to her right. There was someone waiting for her. It was the man I had seen her with when she came to visit her mother that time with the basketball. The man with the trucker's hat, who'd passed over before her. Her grandfather. Shylo's mother had told me they were close, so his presence and support of Shylo made sense.

With gratitude and lightness of being, I looked across to where they were both standing and smiled at her grandfather. They were about to leave. 'Hi, Mum!' remarked Shylo, with a wave that was clearly to be relayed to her mum. Then they both turned and began to walk away.

'Love you, sweetheart!' I replied, now in tears. Shylo's messages were so meaningful, so profound.

26

THE OPPORTUNITY TO LEARN NEVER ENDS

As the days turned into weeks, Shylo's presence and communications became something I treasured. I was so deeply grateful for her interactions. They continued to open up greater dimensions of understanding, drawing me deeper into the level of the soul, into greater truths about life and how to live it.

Summer in Oregon was beautiful. Walking home from my office along quaint streets, past historic homes with large old trees and gardens rich in colour and fragrance, then further up into the mountain where we lived, was always meaningful. With Jessica away visiting her father and friends in Australia, I was able to flow more freely with Shylo's spontaneous visits.

It was midafternoon. I had been standing at our French doors, which looked out across the beautiful Rogue Valley. The computer was on and I was about to start writing, when suddenly I felt Shylo once again burst into my day announcing: 'I want to be heard! I have something to say!'

At that moment, the energy shifted. Another person in spirit had entered. Moments later, a woman in spirit was sitting in the chair to the right of my desk. I recognised her immediately. This was the woman I had often seen with Shylo, in the days immediately after she passed. She was like Shylo's mentor, an elder from the spirit realm, who offered Shylo wisdom and support.

Her grace, love and wisdom touched me. She was so humble, so unaffected. Her powerful presence demonstrated the deep humility and profound simplicity that came with a life lived in service to the awakening of spiritual truth in others. As I sat down at my desk, her communication began.

'I told Shylo her life there was never meant to be a long one. Each soul comes with a blueprint, a map of their life journey ahead, designed and agreed upon before they are born. Shylo had been offered an opportunity to directly influence many in the course of her life. Her learning in part was about the limitations she'd placed on herself by taking her own life, an action that put an end to further opportunities for her to evolve on earth. The essential reason for incarnating on earth is for souls to learn and grow. Yet even her actions that ended her life held value. Through her early departure, Shylo helped others who knew her and loved her to evolve, by experiencing a great sense of loss and the questions it raised. Of course, the higher design is that life never dies but continues on. Shylo continues on.

'Challenges bring the human experience to new levels of awakening. Emotional suffering is often caused by limiting thoughts and unhelpful emotions, arising from unresolved difficulties in life. They render people less able to navigate the storms of life, as circumstances change and emotions rise,' Shylo's mentor explained.

'Many souls begin to thrive after they complete their learning here, awakening to higher understanding and realising greater potential. As souls open up and receive instruction from those around them, who can breathe new life into their challenging moments, their emotional suffering can be eased. By learning how to more effectively deal with life's challenging moments, to let go of what isn't true to self, dormant potential is awakened, bringing order to disorder. This assists these souls in their learning and transition.

'Just as a deeper breath gives rise to release of the breath, freedom from the restrictions of limiting beliefs or simply feeling the love they have been unable to experience, allows a profound release from their suffering. All these assist in bringing about a soul's greater self-understanding, and then their suffering is eased. An experience of belonging, in the sense of discovering a grander vision of what is meaningful, alleviates suffering.

'What we in spirit hope for young people is that they come to know a way of living and operating that releases them from limiting beliefs about who they are, or what they have to be. Instead, they learn how to grow beyond their limitations, by living from the unique perspective of Soul. Remember, when someone passes over, they don't emerge in spirit and say: "Well, maybe next time I can get a new sports car. Or, maybe next time I can end my suffering by living in another city. Or, well I'm so glad I managed to get those 'straight A' results when I was seventeen. That was a great achievement! I could show everyone what great value I was." That is not what a soul learns. That is not the purpose of being incarnate.

'In truth, souls say very different things in the course of their earthly life review. Those of us in spirit would like you to see an experience of someone during their life review,' said Shylo's wise mentor.

The next thing I became aware of was that my consciousness was drawn away from my home, my location, my place in time. In a heartbeat, I was on the 'other side.' Suddenly, I was viewing the experience of a middle-aged woman in her mid-fifties beginning her life review. The woman wore a red dress and thin belt with small buttons down the front. Her wavy brown hair sat just below her shoulders. Within moments, I clearly heard her say: 'As I look back on the life I've just had, the one thing I can see above anything else is that I wasn't able to see my own value. I needed the recognition of others to bring me value. I had to strive for A levels to feel I was more acceptable. I needed to value myself more. I needed to experience a deeper appreciation of just how valuable I already was. I see that now. I see more now than I ever did. If I could have seen that then, I would have done things differently; I could have experienced more, seen more of the world and taken a different pathway. I'm happy I've learnt this now.'

The next moment, I realised the woman was speaking about working with self-worth, now she had passed into spirit. 'I could teach others about what is important, what is really of value,' she volunteered. 'So, if I participated in a class project here, I could support teenagers with a thirst to achieve high results to feel of greater value. Maybe I could help them see that even though I felt like them in the life I've just had, I've since learnt that all this focus on achievement doesn't matter as much as I thought. Had I been able to see my value during my last life, I could have experienced more joy and happiness, less sadness and longing. I see that now. It would be very special to help others see that.'

The woman then smiled such a radiant smile, one that came from somewhere deep within her. She seemed to experience such a feeling of completion and fulfilment during her life review. I could see the depth of healing that had taken place, as she looked back over her life just lived. That profound yet loving process took her to a place of higher elevation, where she accessed greater understanding and wisdom. From that place of awareness, she was able to plan a way forward of higher service, where the sharing of her insights and wisdom could make a real difference to others.

As I sat trying to take in everything I'd seen, I reflected on how meaningful the universe is—how even our perceived mistakes and misunderstandings are never lost. As we change our perception of how we view the things we've done and chosen not to do, they become signposts for us to learn and grow, and then help others on their journey through space and time. Knowing this, I could see there was no place for regret; the important thing was to look for wisdom and opportunities to develop, in life's inevitable ups and downs.

I also knew in that moment that what I had or hadn't done, what I owned or didn't own, was no longer as important. The true value of my life lay in my elevation of consciousness and the wisdom I was gaining, then being able to share that wisdom to make a difference in the lives of others. That was always my intention, my dream. My upcoming trip to Arizona would be one of those special opportunities.

27

WARRIOR SPIRIT

It was always such a joy to visit Sedona. My emotions would always peak the moment Sedona's striking red rocks came into view. It always felt like a homecoming to me. Those amazing rocks are visually and spiritually breathtaking. I never tire of them. Set against the beautiful blue Arizona sky, those majestic red rocks are a reminder of the sacredness of this land and its indigenous keepers.

I was in Sedona at the invitation of Margo and her husband, associates of our beloved Professor John Mack. This generous, engaging couple had supported many, through their vision and commitment to the evolution of our consciousness. One of Margo's passions was to support international education and research into sustainable spiritually-based health and wellbeing. She'd invited me into these discussions and, along with John, I had enthusiastically agreed to participate.

I shared one of the guest houses with Jennifer, an interior designer from northern California, who was planning to create a retreat centre in northern California. Our conversation was effortless. Standing in the kitchen at breakfast, Jennifer began to tell me of the recent death of her 32-year-old son James, a highly-proficient mountaineer and extreme skier. James and three others had been dropped onto a 10,000-foot ridge on

Mount Saint Elias in Alaska, the second highest mountain in America. The group included Paul, a lifelong friend of James and also a highly-experienced skier and climber.

The men began their climb, but soon frostbite and exhaustion saw two of the skiers return back to base, leaving James and Paul to try to make it to the summit on their own. They were close to the summit but the light was fading, making their challenge near impossible. Suddenly, one of the skiers who'd been left on the lower level caught sight of James sliding down the mountain out of control. James fell about 2,000 feet to his death. Paul had fallen too. Both were dead.

The story was clearly painful. As Jennifer took a few slow sips of her coffee, I felt encouraged by Shylo's visits to speak more freely about the world of spirit, to help soften Jennifer's pain. As she stood listening, I began to notice that familiar energy shift in the room. Within moments, a young man in spirit walked in. He had dark hair and a noticeable reserve. He moved forward to stand in front of Jennifer. As I described his features and personality, Jennifer confirmed that this was Paul. I explained that this visit back to earth wasn't easy for him. It was soon made clear that Paul's appearance was for his learning and progression, as well as for Jennifer's benefit.

Within moments, we discovered he had come to honour Jennifer's emotional pain at losing her son James, his climbing partner and closest friend that day on the mountain. Then moments later, Paul turned his head and looked back across the room as a taller young man entered. His love and gentleness were palpable. Through her tears, Jennifer confirmed that this was her son, James.

'James seems to be showing me a bracelet, Jennifer,' I softly shared. 'There seems to be some reason why he wants you to know that he is wearing the bracelet.'

Jennifer sobbed. Then after a while she smiled, with a look of radiance. 'My daughter gave that bracelet to James, just before he left for the trip.

She's only twenty, and she loved him so much. She bought it for him to wear while he was away. It will be so special for her to hear this.'

Within the hour, Jennifer left to return home to San Francisco, promising to keep in touch. I knew that Providence had allowed our paths to meet, to build a healing bridge between worlds, yet again bringing greater understanding.

With a few hours to spare, I was given a ride into town and enjoyed browsing the stores before our evening meetings. It was the music, haunting Native American singing with the beat of those powerful drums that drew me into the store. Its rhythm spoke to my soul. As I touched the feathers and drums on display, I felt something stirring within me, a deep longing for connection and community—for home.

While waiting in San Francisco for my connecting flight back to Oregon the following day, I called Jessica to let her know I would soon be home. Then before boarding, I rang John in Boston, letting him know the outcome of our meetings in Sedona. He told of an upcoming event in Boston he'd organised with a colleague. 'Why don't you come along? You can get up and speak about your work. Think about it. See what you can do about getting here.'

Feeling grateful but unprepared, I graciously declined John's offer and boarded my plane. On this brief flight, the majesty of Mount Shasta heralded the closeness of home. This remarkable snow-capped mountain was always as spectacular from the air as it was from the ground. As I stared out the window mesmerised by its timeless beauty, my thoughts were with Shylo. Her hometown was just over thirty miles south of Mt Shasta, while our hometown Ashland was just over sixty miles north.

The most joyful part of my arrival home was being back with Jessica; to feel the gift of our belonging. After a late dinner together downtown, I was sitting reading some of my journal of Shylo's communications from beyond the veil, when suddenly I was drawn to check my emails.

There was an unexpected email from Shylo's mother, revealing a historically-significant and powerful story embedded in Shylo's ancestry.

Shylo was a direct descendant of Chief Shasteka of the Shasta Nation of Northern California. He was her fifth great grandfather, and one of the leaders of the Shasta Indian tribes who lived in the early 1800s, in the abundance and beauty of the Mount Shasta region.

During the gold rush, new settlers moved onto what had been native land, and Chief Shasteka's people began to starve. In an attempt to save the lives of his tribe, Chief Shasteka led them to resist this new settlement. He was eventually captured and imprisoned in Fort Jones. Refusing to eat, he starved to death. He was survived by his daughters, Mary and Kate, who escaped into the woods and were eventually found and taken care of by European settlers.

As I finished reading this astonishing email, I suddenly felt someone next to me in spirit to my left. At first I couldn't quite see who it was, so I stood up from my desk and stepped away a little. It was then I real-ised it was Shylo, leaning on her elbows, hands under her chin looking at my computer screen. I felt so happy to see her there. Moments later she stepped away, directing me back to the desk. She clearly wanted to communicate, so I took the lead: 'Shylo, I want you to bring your great grandfather, Chief Shasteka, to see me,' I said lightheartedly. 'I want to thank him for having his daughter, Kate, and all your other ancestors, and for then creating you. I want to thank him, because I feel blessed by you, Shylo.' I paused for a moment, then continued: 'Okay, I'm ready. What do you have to share?'

Shylo was now sitting in the chair to the left of my desk. For a moment, things were noticeably quiet and still. I looked to the right of me to see what might be happening. Nothing. But then as I looked to my left, I was struck by the sight of an older Native American with long dark hair and a grey blanket around his shoulders. He was slowly walking into the middle of the room. Stunned, my body was hit by powerful chills, as my mind struggled to take it all in.

'You said you wanted to see him,' said Shylo.

'I didn't know it would be this fast!' I replied, almost unable to breathe.

Chief Shasteka walked towards me with a gentle wisdom and humility, then stopped and simply sat down on the floor. Mesmerised, I sat watching him as he quietly adjusted his blanket, settled and became comfortable. His presence was extraordinary. Another strong wave of chills flowed over the full length of my body.

At that moment, I knew he was connecting with me across the infinite field of space-time—the same way Shylo did. I waited patiently, almost nervously, for him to begin. Within seconds, I could clearly hear him singing. He was singing a prayer, connecting with the Great Spirit to bring blessing on this place and moment of our communication. It was unbelievable. Yet another wave of cold chills flooded over me, as I felt the immensity of his blessing. Without thinking I pulled my sleeves down, as there seemed to be a distinct drop in temperature.

At first his words were simple, almost rudimentary in translation. However, as he became more adept at using me as his vehicle of transla-tion, his statements became more fluid. They ranged more widely, and were more complex too. As his words flowed through me, they brought a special depth to my being, taking me to a place that was sacred and profound. It was my spiritual home.

'They have lost their way,' he began. 'Many people, they cannot see. They have forgotten. Speak to them. Bring lessons to grow in their hearts. Help them come back from starvation, to remember what they have forgotten. Ask them to grow food in the earth, to plant and to harvest what they plant. Tell them to turn the soil and thank the Great Spirit for rain. This brings the rain to make the plants grow. Teach them to make the rain, to ask the rain to bring life to the crops for many to eat.'

As he paused, my heart felt the deeper significance of his message: the disconnection so many of us have with nature, with our land, with the earth.

As Chief Shasteka continued, his focus turned to our disconnection with each other. 'They wanted to destroy us, because of the way we lived,' he said with great sadness. 'They wanted what we had. They broke our spirit and shackled us. They took us away from where we lived. We had no value to them. We were very poor; no longer could we hunt on our land. There was so much suffering. Many died. Much wisdom was buried.'

I could feel the tragedy of the loss of his people; the loss of their wisdom and ancient ways. It was a message our world desperately needed to hear. As the higher truth reminds us all, it is always about choice. The choice we have to make much-needed changes, and the hope we can generate when we make good choices.

'The spirit of our fathers is returning,' he continued, his words flowing easily now. 'We could not live like they live now. It would kill our spirit. Never to go outside, never to hear the elk cry, the wolf howl, to catch the last rays of the sun as it falls behind the mountains. To feel the spirit of the earth and the rivers that gives you food that brings life. This is the richness of life as I knew it, and it is gone. But now we are returning to the starving people with our wisdom, to the ones who have forgotten.'

Then directing his message to me, he said: 'You have come back home to the place where you felt the mountains and the rivers call you, to a way you too had forgotten. The passage of time has taught you to break away from the ways that brought suffering—ways that caused you pain ... so much pain.'

Taking a deep breath to cope with the intensity of his magnificent presence and powerful message, I briefly closed my eyes, waiting for him to continue.

'Many people say they want to find peace. Peace is in the rivers, in the land. It comes from the mountains, from these places, not from things people have, but from the place that is left when the things people have are taken from them. What is left is where they find peace. It is in the sky. It is already there. When they take away their things, they see the sky. They see the trails through the mountains. They follow where the trail leads them. The richness is inside. Then their hearts sing to the rivers, to the land, to the mountains. It takes them away from the places where there was no peace. It leads them home ...'

Seconds passed; Chief Shasteka was now silent. I looked across to the place on the floor where he'd been sitting, and he was no longer there. I wondered if he had gone. Looking at my computer screen, I realised it was almost 11pm. Then suddenly, moments later, I turned back to see the Chief was there, standing up now and moving closer. At first, he stared down at my computer screen. I wondered what he would make of it. Then he turned and looked directly at me. His presence and wisdom felt immense. I was overwhelmed by his presence, by such majesty and deep humility.

I waited, still and attuned. His powerful gaze stared deep into my being. For some moments, he just stood and stared. My heart was hushed and reverent. He drew his blanket a little closer across his chest. Then, with great strength and heart, he spoke to me and through me to all those who would listen: 'Ask your people: when there is no more fish left to hunt, when the rivers are too sick to hold food, when the trail is lost into the mountains, when will it be enough? When will they have enough? What will there be left? People are sick, because they have lost their spirit. Bring them home.'

28

JOHN'S
HOMECOMING

It was late afternoon in September 2004. I had taken a walk in a very beautiful local park and, as always, felt replenished by the magnificent trees there. As I stopped in front of a very old redwood in the centre of the park, I thought back to Shylo's car wreck exactly three years ago. With my hand resting against the tree, feeling its wisdom and strength, I reflected about how pivotal that single moment had been for Shylo. I pondered how often unexpected events in life have the power and potential to alter us most.

Back home, I briefly called in on a neighbour just three doors down. As we stood chatting at his front door, I noticed Jessica running down the street towards me. 'You have a call. It's serious, Mum. You have to come! Now! It's Maria from Boston. Something has happened.'

Maria worked at the Centre for Psychology and Social Change in Cambridge, and had welcomed me with great warmth from the moment I arrived in Boston. I'd come to know her as a dedicated loyal supporter of Professor John Mack's work and vision. She too was committed to the pursuit of a greater understanding of our extraordinary human experience.

Running as quickly as we could back to the house, I picked up the phone. 'Elizabeth sweetie, it's Maria,' her soft voice was obviously emotional. 'I have some bad news,' she continued. 'John was killed tonight in London.'

The news was surreal, incomprehensible. John was like a father, especially since my own father had passed two years before. What would our lives be like without him?

'As soon as the call came through from London, I just had to call you before anybody else. You came straight into my mind.' Maria's voice was vulnerable, revealing the depth of emotion she was now feeling. 'I'm so sorry to have to tell you such devastating news. There's another call coming through, so I will call you back as soon as I can,' Maria said.

Placing the phone beside me, I sobbed uncontrollably. 'What is it?' asked Jessica. 'What's happened?' Trying my best to compose myself, I shared the traumatic news, then asked if she was okay. She looked down into her hands, silently nodding.

After a while, a kaleidoscope of visions began to flood into my mind's eye. I saw John's face filled with joy and elation. He was literally brimming with wonderment and enthusiasm. He seemed so excited to finally see and sense the greater reality of life. I thought about the many times I had shared my multi-sensory experiences of what existed beyond our everyday world with John. Now he was seeing it, experiencing it all with his own senses.

It was these same expanded realities that he had explored and researched, as a pioneer thinker and visionary. Across the world, many people with extraordinary experiences felt supported and validated by John's belief in the existence of these greater realities. John had become a father figure to many. With a tremendous mind and high integrity, he held such enthusiasm and a commitment to truth. Those who came to know John couldn't help but hold him in high esteem. His loss would be deeply felt.

Before long the phone rang. It was my actor friend, Mark, who was highly intuitive. Our paths had crossed some months before. When I shared the devastating news, he offered me such comfort and understanding. 'John is so happy,' he assured me. 'I can see him like a kid in a candy store. I sense he's going to be working with you. He'll be part of your new life path.'

Hearing another call on the line, we cut our conversation short. It was Maria from Boston again. 'I've had more news,' she began. 'I was just told that John was a pedestrian. He was hit crossing the road. He must have just stepped off a kerb, not looking the right way in London traffic. That's all I know right now.'

I was shattered by this horrific news. But then, within seconds, I began to feel lightness and a distinct presence in the room. I told Maria of a sudden deep sense of sacredness, of love and light pervading the air. It was almost as if the very particles of air swirled and shifted around me. This wasn't any ordinary stirring of the atmosphere. It was a transcendent, transformational moment, a shift in time and place.

'Maria,' I gasped. 'I'm feeling a lot of pain in my right arm now, my right shoulder too. And my head is feeling strange ... I sense John was impacted on the right side of his body.' With more and more pain and sensation flooding my arm, shoulder and head, I told Maria: 'I think he's here. I think John's coming in.'

Within moments John stepped forward, resplendent in the most brilliant light. His face was radiant and he was clearly eager to share his new world. The love and appreciation I felt for him overwhelmed me. His visit was so precious, a blessing.

It was then I heard his voice: 'If it's too much for you, then I can stop,' he assured me. He could obviously see and sense the physical pain I was going through, communicating with him so soon after his accident.

'No, I'm okay John. It's okay. I'm just so happy you are here,' I insisted. 'It's so wonderful to see you again.'

Choking with tears, I placed the palm of my right hand against my heart, as a vision of a candle with a softly focused flame came into my mind's eye. Accompanying this lovely image came the insight that, as the flame burns lower, the energy is not lost. It simply changes form.

John no longer required the learning experience that his earthly body had provided. He would no longer be compromised or restricted by that limited physical form. He was leaving the experience of the earth plane, transcending this space and time, returning to a form and fashion that enabled him to access unlimited knowledge, experience, non-locality and unity of consciousness. He was overwhelmed with the clarity of understanding he had now in spirit—everything he could see from that side of the veil. He explained that it was as if he had been living with frosted glasses on here in the physical plane, but now he didn't need glasses at all. Through this shift in perspective, he had fully awakened to his power. The feeling was clearly extraordinary for him.

'There's no longer anything to separate him from fully understanding and experiencing everything as it truly is,' I told Maria, who was still listening on the other end of the phone. 'This is why he feels so enthusiastic, why he's come through so soon.'

John explained that he'd chosen to pass over in England, as it had been significant in his soul history. For him, it was a place of mystery and legend. In my mind's eye there came a clear vision of Stonehenge. I was told that Stonehenge is an inter-dimensional portal, an open entry point to another dimension. So for John, England was the passageway he chose to take from this dimension to the next.

'I'm frightened,' said Maria timidly. She explained that the table lamp had suddenly and unexpectedly just gone out in her Boston apartment. Aware of her vulnerability, I gently reassured her that she was truly safe, and that what was happening was indeed very powerful and significant.

Before long, the pain once again overtook my arm. My shoulder and head were worst of all. I winced then cried, feeling the intensity and severity of the impact on John's body at the point of collision. At the same time, John moved back and disappeared from the room. Almost at once, the intensity of pain in my shoulder and arm diminished dramatically.

Within seconds, I could sense someone else in spirit move towards me and sit on the end of the bed facing me. 'It's Shylo!' I whispered to

Maria. I was amazed and touched to see Shylo's role as intermediary in John's transition. I listened with reverence, as Shylo explained that John was now being supported in spirit in his 'convalescing' phase. He was being assisted to 'find his feet' and become used to his new surroundings. Yet even at this very early stage of adjustment, John had been so eager to share his new insights.

Shylo gently explained that it would take some time before his energy had fully emerged on the other side, to allow him to more readily interact with those on this side of the veil.

Having fulfilled her role in explaining what was happening to John, Shylo left. Not only was I confronted by the shocking reality of John's unexpected death, I was struggling to integrate his reappearance. Maria and I decided to continue our conversation at a later point. Having said our goodbyes I remained where I sat, crying and reflecting and crying some more.

Walking back into the living room to join Jessica, I was struggling to contain my intense emotional pain. 'John wouldn't like you to cry,' said Jessica. 'You know very well we'll get to see him more now than when he lived in Boston. He will be in our house, instead of us living with him in his house. Instead of me creeping up behind him as he played his piano, he can now creep up behind me as I practise my guitar.'

'I know,' I replied. 'But I just can't help feeling sad. I loved him so much, and I feel this is such a tragedy. He's a man with so much life and wisdom; he's done so much for so many people and now he can't be here anymore.'

'But he is here!' she insisted. 'He will be here more now than before!'

It was another 24 hours before I would truly realise how right Jessica was.

29

CROSSING OVER

I had a dull pain in my right arm and shoulder for some hours, and found myself having to rub my arm to soothe the pain. As the pain increased, it would usually signal John's entry.

At 12.30am, I was sitting at my computer recording the previous hour's events, when suddenly I saw John enter the room. 'It's wonderful. No matter what anybody tells you, it's like nothing you could ever understand until you see it, feel it,' he explained. 'I want you to write down what I tell you. I want you to tell the others I'm fine. I arrived safely. I've come to the right place,' he added, with his typical dry sense of humour. 'The others seemed to find me where I was. They were there waiting for me as I was catapulted out of my physical body. I could clearly see them around me. They must have already been there waiting for me. I hadn't time to even think about what had happened ...'

The very next moment I was taken on a spectacular journey into the wonderment of John's passing over into 'creation.' Instantly, we were transported into a mesmerising, luminescent, all-enveloping, light-filled space. It was magnificent, captivating and intoxicating. The light seemed to envelop you, to merge with you and draw you into its radiant loving consciousness. This light was imbued with understanding, knowledge and wisdom. It had an ecstatically beautiful quality about it.

John's eyes radiated love, gentleness and humility. I could see and feel the grandeur of his passage, his reverence for what he beheld. He was encircled by angels' voices in celestial song, heralding his blessed return as he moved along the passageway between worlds. Those around him congratulated him for the divine work he had done on the earth plane. There was a feeling of great reverence for his contribution, his high service to humanity. John seemed in awe of this spectacle. His face was soft and filled with love.

My arm was still hurting, and I felt dazed with exhaustion. I needed to sleep. Then just as suddenly, I was out of the experience of John's passing, and back in my own terrible grief at his passing. Respite came with sleep at 3am.

I was woken at 7.15am. Jessica was preparing to leave for school. As she walked over to me, I held out my arms to hug her, longing for the comfort of our embrace. 'I'm so sad about John,' I began, wrestling with insistent tears.

'I'm going to leave for school soon, Mum. Make sure you eat something,' she replied, safely contained inside her own world.

The day became a blur of grief and sadness, with many phone calls to and from people all over the country. Throughout the day when I was not on the phone, I would receive random images of John, or what seemed to relate to him. One image was of The Beatles' *Abbey Road* album cover, with the four band members on a pedestrian crossing, one behind the other. I had little idea at that point that John had actually been killed while walking across a pedestrian crossing.

Late in the afternoon, as I sat in numbed silence at my computer waiting for an acquaintance, I opened my laptop and read an email from Shylo's mother. She had written to ask how I was. She noted that John had been fatally knocked down exactly three years to the day that Shylo had had her near-fatal car accident.

Suddenly, I felt the same distinct pain down my right arm and knew immediately it was John. Within moments, I saw him vividly with my psychic vision. He motioned for me to write: 'It's hell trying to get through to you. You're so busy. Can we make a specific time to communicate?' he asked.

I could see and hear John so clearly, I found myself talking to him as I normally would: 'Okay ... well, can we make it 7pm? But how does that actually work for you? How would you even know when it's 7pm here?'

Not one to be caught up in anything trivial, he briskly responded: 'It doesn't matter. I have some things I wanna talk to you about.'

At that point I felt his energy dissipate, and my arm return to normal. He was gone. Quickly replying to the email from Shylo's mum, I shared my profound grief at John's passing, then left to do the family shopping downtown.

Within minutes of my return home, I received a call from Shylo's mother who lovingly acknowledged my loss. She had only just discovered John's research and book on teenage suicide. 'It's all connected, isn't it?' she asked, with a spiritual knowing I was so impressed by.

After the call, I walked into the living room and glanced up at the kitchen clock. It was 6.40pm. I had twenty minutes until my meeting with John, and yet this was the first time all day that I could spend time with Jessica. We sat on the sofa watching TV, talking a little, but mostly just sharing one another's company.

Before long I saw John nearby, with his usual 'getting down to business' look. Glancing briefly at my wristwatch, I noticed it was 6.55pm. Gently explaining to Jessica that 'Mr. John' had asked me to make time to communicate with him, I assured her it wouldn't take too long. 'I love you,' I said, leaning over to tenderly kiss her on the head as she sat watching television.

Then as I began to walk away from her, I noticed a light appear next to her on the couch. It was my father, smiling and watching TV beside her. 'Fardie is here!' I whispered reassuringly, as I walked away from her and over towards the stairs. It was so like my father to want to be with her when I couldn't, to be supportive. He was such a loving dad.

Looking back over towards Jessica as I descended the stairs, I was caught between a desire to stay and share time with her, and my call to higher service. 'I love you Dad!' I called, as I disappeared into my bedroom below and closed the door.

My bedroom was aglow with the light of the setting sun, its soft hue creating a sacred space around me. The pale blue sky and pinkish white clouds, with the pine trees poised in silent reverence, gently marked the passing of the day, and the passing of this great man, my beautiful friend. 'Just stay with the flow; write it as I tell you, but stay with the flow,' John began, in his usual commanding, lovable, Harvard professor way.

'Okay, John. You're on!' I said, reaching for my bottle of water and taking a much-needed gulp.

There was a distinct alteration to the energy in the room, as my bedroom was now 'merged' into John's office. John was sitting relaxed at what appeared to be his desk in his home in Cambridge. I suddenly became aware of a feeling of tightness in his throat, a distinct feeling of sadness.

'Leaving behind those you love ain't so easy,' John began. 'It's not so much that you can't see them or feel them. It's being out of it, away from what's happening, that's hard. That's why this form of communication is so vital, to be the bridge, so people like you can be a conduit to those of us here. That's so important, it's so important.'

'I'm struggling with tears now, John. I'm sad you had to go and I'm sad you had ... I'm just sad,' I shared.

'I know, I know,' he gently replied, as he looked through papers, his glasses perched on the bridge of his nose. 'I can't be there now. I had to be here. This is where I need to be right now. This is important. This is where I have to be.'

'I get the distinct impression that where you are right now is a new office you have created, there in your new dimension. It looks identical to your bedroom office in Cambridge. Yet I get the feeling you are not in your actual home,' I commented, trying to understand where he seemed to be.

'You're right. I'm here. Now, where were we?' he replied abruptly, obviously focused on what he intended to share. 'Okay, here it is. What I want to do right now is give you a rudimentary guide to my journey here, to demonstrate what happened.'

'John, I don't know why, but it's just become a little hard to hear you,' I interjected.

'Let me turn up the volume then,' he responded, reaching down to what appeared to be an amplifier, perhaps metaphorically inferring he could make adjustments from his side, to optimise our communication.

'Everything here happens faster than there. Time's a lot slower where you are, so when you come here, you need to get used to the new speed or vibration that you process, and the time it takes for things to occur,' John continued.

'Okay,' I replied. 'I'm seeing a vision of walkways at an airport and how tricky it is when you walk onto a moving walkway from the slower pace you've been going. Suddenly, you're experiencing your movement at a quickened pace. Then getting off at the other end, it feels odd to be walking normally again—like you are actually walking at an even slower pace than you were before. Is that how it is?' I asked.

'This is going to take a long time to get down, if you're going to type it!' John said, impatiently.

'John, I'm being shown a vision of your tape recorder, which you used for interviews for your work. I will try to procure one from somewhere. I know you are keen to work quickly on this, but for now this is the way it will have to be. I will type as quickly as I can,' I replied, playfully adding: 'You were impatient this side of the veil, John. But you will just have to cope with it now. See how empowered I am with you now?' I said, enjoying the interaction.

'My passing has worked wonders already. I can see that much,' he quipped, with a wry smile. He was craning forward, as if looking at something. I realised it was a clock. 'Right. How are we doing for time here?' he asked.

Almost thirty minutes of real time had passed. I had the feeling John was taking into consideration that Jessica was on her own upstairs—well, with my father in spirit there with her. 'I think we have a little time John,' I replied, holding hope this wasn't going to be the end of our interaction. But as I looked up, John was gone from his desk. Our communication had ceased for now, so I eagerly returned to Jessica.

It was 10pm when I discovered another email message with more detail of John's death. The media reports were claiming that John had been killed by a drunk driver, while using a pedestrian crossing. This news confirmed the reason for my vision of The Beatles *Abbey Road* cover. The police had arrested the driver who had caused John's death. Family, international friends, colleagues and supporters of John were all in shock, stunned, angered, or suspicious about his tragic death.

Meanwhile, here in my home in Oregon, John continued his interactions. He did not focus on how he died, but on what contribution he could make to the understanding of our limited concept of death, and the reality of life beyond the death of the body, the soul's physical vehicle. He was now ensconced in his new office in 'creation' and ready to continue his important work from the other side.

It was almost beyond me to cope with the two worlds simultaneously. I was drawn to stay with the higher story I was now privileged to participate in. I now knew, without any doubt, that John's life and work was to continue beyond the death of his physical body.

It was 11.15pm and I'd set up my laptop and printer on our small antique dining table in the living room. This, it seemed, was to become my new writing desk. John suddenly walked into the room and seated himself on the couch. He was more informally dressed, a cup of coffee in one hand and a baked treat in the other. It was so like the many moments we'd had in his home in Cambridge. It warmed my heart.

'We have to have regular contact to make this happen,' he announced. 'So I will be here while you are at home and Jessica is at school. We have lots to do. I really want to bring a whole new level of insight to people through you. Time to ruffle some more feathers,' he said, with his familiar, wise, enthusiastic smile.

'I'm tired, John. I think I'm going to have to go to bed. I love you and I miss you being here, and I am so grateful that you have come to me to communicate. I feel so enormously blessed,' I replied, feeling sad yet comforted by his presence.

The next morning I woke to the sound of my alarm clock. It was 9am. Normally I would have woken earlier, or been woken by Jessica getting ready for school. I walked into Jessica's room to find her bedroom empty. She had left without saying goodbye. Reluctantly, I left my downstairs bedroom and climbed the stairs to the living room, noticing a distinctly different energy from the previous day. There was a sense of peace; the calm after the storm. My body felt exhausted and heavy, yet I also felt a sense of relief.

Switching on my computer I had a significant number of emails, some forwarded from John's office in Boston. As I began to wade through them, there were several letters from people in London. One wrote of the horror and injustice of John's death. Another shared the conversation about life after death they'd had with John, on the very afternoon of his passing. Another email contained an article from *The Boston Globe* entitled: 'Pulitzer winner is killed in accident.' Once again, the grim reality of John's death confronted me.

The anguish and grief expressed by the media and John's friends was in stark contrast to the enthusiasm and buoyancy John was experiencing in spirit. Trying to cope with the intensity of this situation, I decided to just acknowledge people's reactions, but not allow myself to be drawn into them. It was self-preservation really. My focus needed to be on the work at hand—to reveal the greater reality of life and its continuance beyond the death of the physical body.

Given my grief and exhaustion, I toyed with the idea of postponing my next client's appointment. But for reasons yet to be discovered, I felt I needed to follow through with my client's session, in spite of feeling so depleted.

Once I was ready for work, I stepped out into the fresh air and was inspired by the sheer natural beauty of the surrounding mountains and the majestic trees along my path. Walking briskly down the hill and across the few blocks to my office, I was surprised to notice John eagerly following. I was suddenly struck by a feeling of trepidation. Being in spirit now meant he could sit in on my work and witness my work as a therapist. At that same moment, I also felt the joy of his presence.

There was no doubt I was stepping into the unknown with John. I'd no idea where the weeks and months ahead would lead me, other than having a distinct feeling my life was about to change beyond recognition.

TWO-WAY MIRROR

Nestled in the comfort of the leather recliner chair in my small upstairs office, I took a few moments to settle my new client, Jennifer, by talking about how I worked, and the sort of things she might experience during our session.

'Before we begin, I just want to explain that the information I receive will come in many ways. I see visually, which we might call 'second sight.' I hear information telepathically and receive messages directly from the 'knowing field.' I might be given information from those in spirit. I can intuitively locate unexpressed emotional debris from past trauma held in your body, and then tune into the information and story it represents. The information may come as a knowing or an experience of a previous event. My awareness can move to other space-time locations we might refer to as past lives, currently impacting your present life. I can also work with you energetically, but I don't have to touch you. It's all about assisting your empowerment, your liberation from whatever is holding you back. Basically, it's the whole shebang that I get. Is that okay?' I asked, adjusting the cushion at the back of my chair.

Jennifer's face lit up with a radiant smile. 'That's great!'

'You could say I'm very forensic in my approach, kind of like Sherlock Holmes, detecting what needs to be understood and released here,'

I continued, laughing a little and feeling the joy of being able to awaken and inspire others. I then added: 'The information comes in very quickly. If I hesitate, it can start to back up like traffic on the LA 405 freeway, so I will go right ahead and begin.'

Already I was noticing a powerful build-up of energy. 'Okay. The first thing I'm noticing is that there's quite a lot of stuck energy, emotional debris in your legs, especially in your upper thighs, your hips and up under your waist. There is deep sadness stored there, a feeling of being unloved. It's a belief that you feel inadequate in some way. It's also indicating you have been restricted in your creative expression during your life; in doing what you truly want to do. These two themes often tend to tie in.

'You have patterns of giving too much to others, after not getting your emotional needs met as a child. You've come to see yourself as less important. Your soul history indicates the same theme there in other lifetimes, so this is an old pattern for you. This pattern is active in your life right now, and this is why it's time to finally place yourself and your own needs first.

'I'm being drawn to your head. I'm seeing you have a tendency to rework things in your mind, keeping things to yourself, instead of letting them go or sharing them with others. You believe other people's ideas, thoughts or desires are more important than yours. These old beliefs keep you stuck. They're unproductive. You also tend to worry about the past and the future, so you miss out on this moment, where we are most powerful. Does this resonate so far?'

Jennifer's eyes flashed wide as she quickly replied: 'You're absolutely correct.' All I had been told prior to the session was that Jennifer was unsure how to move her life forward, and was seeking clarity in her personal and professional life.

'It's really important in this time of great change for you to take care of yourself and make time for your own needs. You have a tendency to attend to your own needs last, and that's because you got the message as a child that you were not worthy. It's time for things to grow and blossom for you. Your inner self needs to be shown she is worthy of love and attention.

'I'm seeing your little inner-child self as a small baby, and you really need to nurture her now. She is wrapped in pink. The colour feels warm and safe and nurturing to her, and I see that your new default pattern to cultivate is to be aware of her and her needs going forward, and to make them a priority. I see you saying to another person: "Yes, I hear what you need, and yet I can't be there right now, but I will see you tomorrow and we can discuss it then," rather than overlooking your baby self and attending to the needs of others. You are a great friend to many people. You give yourself to others too readily. Now is the opportunity to reflect and review how much you have placed others' needs before your own and, in doing so, limited the choices you've made for yourself. This life you have is actually for **you**. You are worthy to live it. Does this make sense?'

'Yes, it does!' Jennifer replied with conviction.

'You know, it's like this: it's as if our spirit guides are sitting in the front row of the theatre, watching us make limiting choices and take self-sabotaging actions in our lives. When we repeat and repeat these same behaviours that are so dishonouring of ourselves, it must be really amazing for them to watch,' I said smiling, moving the session into a more aware, awake perspective. 'It's like I see them sitting there watching this story of our unconscious patterns of behaviour, where we get stuck just repeating the same thing. Our spirit guides must be wondering how long it's going to be till the movie changes, till we actually wake up and realise that this life is so incredibly precious, and we are so incredibly important! It's like: hello universe! I'm finally listening!' I shared, inviting Jennifer to join in the laughter with me.

'We all do this, Jennifer, which is why we really need to get this stuff sorted; wake up from the limiting programming, where we're almost asleep at the wheel. Then we can become the glorious versions of ourselves that we have the potential to be!'

With some lightness and fun to further encourage Jennifer's growth in awareness, the session continued.

'Okay. So I'm sensing what it was like for you at the age of eight ... between seven and eight, but closer to turning eight. I sense a great loss, a significant change. Your life situation seemed to worsen. Your needs were met even less. I'm being shown this really impacted on you, because that was when you really cemented the belief that you were not enough, that your own needs were not important. Does this make sense?'

'Oh sure,' Jennifer affirmed. 'My parents separated when I was about seven and a half, so I remember how different my eighth birthday was. My father left the state to take another job. We didn't get to see him much after that. My mother had to go back to work, so things were really different from that point onwards,' Jennifer shared, with real sadness.

It was then I became aware that we were not alone. Sitting just behind me to my left I could clearly see and sense John, eagerly listening in. Continuing the consultation, information flowed through me as usual. Jennifer continued to listen and verify my insights with enthusiasm.

Suddenly, unexpectedly, I began to hear John commenting on what he could see, eager to share his insights with me. However in doing so, he was inadvertently drawing my energy and focus away from Jennifer, as I listened to him telepathically. I tried to listen to him, but my client was talking at the same time, so I couldn't concentrate. I was worried that I would be distracted. After a while, I sensed he realised how challenging this was for me, and he suddenly stopped sharing his insights.

As the session continued, I was shown further into significant situations in Jennifer's childhood and teenage years, and more detail of limiting past life patterns. As always, this older and deeper level of information provided Jennifer with deep insight and guidance into the hidden resistance that was holding her back from moving more fully into her own personal power and life potential.

'As we've highlighted your underlying psycho-spiritual story, the shift at the cellular level of your being is already starting to take place,'

I commented. It was essential I was able to reach Jennifer at a cellular level, as this is where toxic attitudes and patterns embed themselves, disempowering us, potentially creating illness. 'We are going to move in now to use energy and direct telepathic connection, to create an immediate cellular response. This means we're basically going to reprogram your cellular consciousness,' I continued. 'This will help you disconnect from the old patterns in this life and other lives, which have caused you to miss out on all the opportunities available to you. These old patterns are why you choose not to stand out and express your own beliefs and ideas, living instead in the shadow of others.'

'It's true,' Jennifer replied reflectively. 'Let's just get in there and change it.'

Jennifer closed her eyes and took a deep breath. It was then I felt an immediate mind and energy connection to her. I raised my right hand up from the chair and the energy transmission began. A warm, powerful flow of energy streamed through my hand towards her, as I merged with her cellular consciousness at a quantum level, to clear her old limiting script.

Jennifer was a psychiatric nurse seeking a more fulfilling way of working and living, and a better understanding of her life ahead. She had been working with a team of psychiatrists in the mental health field in California, but she now desired a more holistic and soulful way of assisting others to grow and heal. The fact that John, as a psychiatric specialist himself, chose to witness this particular session with Jennifer was a very interesting point of synchronicity.

Without forewarning, I suddenly experienced a strong deep pain in the upper part of my right arm. Announcing to Jennifer that I needed to pause for a moment, I simply explained that some information was being given to me from someone who was observing our interaction from the spirit world. I sat and waited in silence, gently rubbing my right arm, which was now significantly painful.

The information flowed into my mind as clear knowing: 'I'm being told the setting where you work is stifling for you, as the insights and broader understanding you often have about various clients differs greatly from those held by the psychiatrists you work with.'

'Yes, that's absolutely right,' Jennifer replied.

'I am being told that you need to understand that psychiatry as it stands is limited, and is headed for huge change. You are also headed for a time of transition from the way you work, and you are being guided now to trust your intuition and higher understanding, and not be intimidated by the limited views of those you work with. You will eventually move from where you are and work in a very different way. Does this make sense to you?'

Jennifer responded with great enthusiasm, confirming she had indeed found it very frustrating that traditional psychiatry seemed so limited. She had also been considering moving from the mainstream practice where she worked to another more holistic group further south, with a more integrative approach which she resonated with.

I felt such deep joy at having John assist me in this way. I knew John wanted to encourage Jennifer, as he did so many worldwide. He was way-showing her how to be a part of the new emerging vision for mental health, with a deeper understanding of the full spectrum of human experience.

John was a visionary scholar dedicated to social change and trans-formation through the expansion of consciousness. Now on the other side of the veil, he was still actively championing the existence of alternative realities beyond the blinkered beliefs still held by so many.

Finishing the session, I hugged Jennifer goodbye. Locking the office door behind me, I made my way down the narrow winding staircase from the cosy third-floor office I shared with a local child psychologist. Along the landing, I walked past the open office of well-known energy medicine expert and author, Donna Eden. Once out of the building, I slowly walked home, comforted by the surrounding trees on East Main Street.

Before long, my legs began to feel leaden. John had already left. I missed him so much. Rounding the corner, I looked across the road to the town cemetery, a sombre reminder of John's passing.

LIGHT BEARER

Arriving home, I sat down at my computer and felt compelled to begin writing. Within a couple of minutes, I received images of the office my dad used to work in—my dad's 'calling-card'—letting me know he was here. Glancing up from the computer screen, I saw him standing in the kitchen as if ready to fix me lunch. 'Oh hey, Dad, it's so lovely that you are here with me,' I said affectionately.

It was then I heard him gently suggest I have some tucker, Australian slang for food. 'Some of your mum's salmon curry would be the shot,' he suggested.

'That's a great idea, Dad,' I replied, my heart filling with love. 'I'll make a curry. Thanks, Dad!'

With that he left, and I became instantly reabsorbed in my task at hand.

It was several more hours before I finally realised I did need to eat something. Minimising the file on my screen, I perused the internet and was back in the dramatic reaction to the ending of John's life. I was battered by the blitz of stories in newspapers and from organisations across the world surrounding his death. But when I pulled up an article titled *John Mack is Dead*, I broke down emotionally.

I had been shielded by beautiful communications from John that honoured the continuation of life, following the death of his physical body. This was the new area of research John had been passionately drawn to, before what many believed was his untimely departure. His new work and passion surrounded the evidence of survival beyond death of well-respected psychiatrist and researcher, Elisabeth Targ.

I suddenly remembered our meaningful conversation that night in his beautiful cottage in Vermont, when he said his new research was perhaps preparing him for his own life's end. There was so much to take in. Suddenly overcome by it all, I buried my face in my hands and sobbed, not sure that I was strong enough to continue to walk between worlds. I wasn't sure I was the best ambassador for John's ongoing work. It was a huge job to try to expand people's narrow views around life and what lies beyond it.

The phone rang moments later. It was my actor friend, Mark. I couldn't help but pour out my feelings to him. With great kindness he offered insight and support, to help me overcome my moment of self-doubt. 'I know you are really going through a lot right now, but those on the other side really, really need you to see yourself as capable and ready, as being worthy to do this,' he stressed. 'And now John is assisting you from over that side, wanting to support you and wanting to continue his wonderful, important work. He has chosen you as the vehicle for that right now, even though you are still struggling with his choosing you.'

Mark was right. The call ended moments later. As I sat back and took a deep breath, my eyes fell on the photo of John on my desk. I placed it on the mantelpiece, beside Jessica's sculpture. Then I took out John's Pulitzer Prize-winning book, *A Prince of our Disorder*, and placed it under the bottom of the photograph. I sensed strongly there was still something to put on top of the book, finally realising it was my stone scarab beetle. As I stood back and reflected on my small monument to John, I sensed there was deeper meaning in the symbol of the scarab beetle. I felt it had to do with John and his passing, and the continuance of his life on the other side.

Researching the internet, I was reminded that the ancient Egyptians referred to the scarab beetle as self-creation and resurrection. The scarab beetle was worshiped as Khepri, 'he who has come into being,' a creator-god. And, just as the scarab beetle pushed a ball of dung before it, the Egyptians imagined that Khepri rolled the sun (the solar ball) across the sky each day. So they regarded Khepri as a form of the sun-god and, hence, an important symbol of creation, resurrection and everlasting life.

It was midnight before I sat down at my desk again. Within seconds, I heard from John.

'I have several things to say to you regarding your session this morning. I saw so much more and was able to understand certain aspects that were dramatically different from the normal interactions a counsellor or any average person would have with someone. What was so fascinating to me, from where I am now and from all I can finally see, was the greater efficiency of time and effectiveness of the intervention process you use. Your abilities enabled Jennifer to move into a true healing process much more quickly and effectively than many in mainstream circles. There was no effort for you to be with her in the way you were, in locating and establishing her issues and magnifying their source. By using your heightened abilities, you were able to bring about significant shifts for her ... not only within her consciousness, but I saw how you were able to directly alter the composition of the cellular mind. That was fascinating to watch.

'As you worked with her, there was no sense of you being controlling; it was the total opposite of that. I see you creating a natural authentic unfolding, totally honouring the existence of alternative realities ... then how these realities can be accessed, bringing the mind and body into balance. It's truly something. I don't believe I ever really saw this to the degree I do now.'

It was wonderful to have John validate my work in this way, yet I felt a sudden sadness in him. 'What's the sadness I can feel, John?' I gently asked.

'I wonder ... I can't say that I regret anything I did. I know that all of what I experienced in my life was to acquire greater knowledge, to impart wisdom, and attain a higher spiritual truth. I realise that ... just between you and me, I guess that in being with you today and sharing the depth and breadth of your own abilities and the impact they have, I just question how things could have been for me if I had been able to do that,' he replied.

Feeling such love and reverence for John, I calmly replied: 'You know I always told you that your role here this time was one of Lightbearer, of coming from a grounded, academic perspective that ultimately brought such credibility to the realities people like me experience. If you had seen and sensed as I do, I don't believe you would have achieved all you did. I know it was an endless frustration to you that you didn't ever see or sense like I can, but you know your work and your life and that all you achieved here was enormously appreciated. That's why your welcome home back to 'creation' was so meaningful.'

I waited for John's reply. I could no longer see him or sense him as I had before. After a while, I used my higher vision and tuned in to 'see' where he had gone. I could see him lying in bed reading, just as in his bedroom in the Cambridge house, his bedside lamp creating a small sphere of light around him. I saw myself lean forward and gently kiss him on the cheek.

As I did so, my perspective suddenly changed. I saw myself through John's eyes instead. Then he gently spoke to me: 'I know how this is for you and how you feel about my death, and about coming here and doing all that you have to do. I want you to know that I feel this is right for you now. It's the right path for you, to open up all your work.'

The next thing I knew I was being shown John's slippers and dressing-gown, a picture of him much older. He was feeble and requiring assistance to walk and shower. 'Better that I am here now and left there strong and healthy, than to wait for life to come to that,' John continued, adding: 'You better get some rest. We're going to be doing some more work tomorrow.'

The very next moment I received a vision of Jessica. 'Jessica just needs things to return to normal,' John shared. 'She just needs to know that everything is going to be the same; that things will go on as normal. She doesn't want to hear about all this stuff, it unsettles her. Don't talk to her about me being here so much, only if you really feel she can cope with it. It's you who needs to quicken the pace a bit and come to terms with the fact I'm here now and that it's okay, as that's how things have to be now. Don't lecture Jessica; just let her be and do what she wants, so that she feels that her environment is stable and normal.'

'I appreciate your support and insight, John,' I replied.

'Okay goodnight,' he said, in his usual gentle way.

Awash with a sense of sacredness of the moment, I sat with my chin in my hands, elbows atop my desk. Below the surface, however, I felt such sadness—like I had lost my father. And I knew I was just one of many who felt this way about John's passing. Yet our connection would remain through the heart, which is able to transcend time and space.

As I contemplated this, I became aware of a beautiful higher energy and such love. A 'message' suddenly streamed into my awareness, revealing that the heart is not just an organ that circulates blood to the body. It spoke of the heart as an active portal, a vital doorway through which we can transcend the incessant workings of the mind, and enter into a state of our truest, highest potential. It revealed a conscious choice we could make, that would eventually lead us to the gentle, fragrant garden of the heart. The message spoke of living from the heart in service to others, allowing them a true reflection of themselves that was real and unending. Living from a place that was always aware of a divine connection with the infinite field of higher knowing and boundless love, where we can experience divine union beyond a sense of separation of any kind.

I could see that by letting go of all the limitations of the mind, we can drop with ease and simplicity into our hearts, opening the gateway to living in a state of grace and higher purpose.

With each passing day, I was being called home to my heart. As I switched off the lights and looked out across the valley, I knew without any doubt that our connection with those we love remains forever.

32

REBIRTH

It was only days since John's fatal accident. Though I could see this from a higher perspective, I was still exhausted from the shock and grief. In between were uplifting moments with John or Shylo. But the constant late nights communicating with them had become extremely taxing. After consulting with a client in the early afternoon, I returned home and began work once more on the transcripts of their communications through the veil.

As the afternoon passed, I realised I had moved into a significant new emotional space, with a tangible feeling of centredness. With it came a lessening of emotional suffering. I was in a more authentic, unattached state of surrender. By following the divine prompting to move from my mind to dwell within my heart, I had come home to the sanctuary of my soul: that wise, peaceful place inside, where there was more of an acceptance of the grace unfolding in my life. It had brought me comfort and release from suffering.

I received a phone call from another close friend in Boston. We talked about the many people she and I were both hearing from, since John's accident and passing. With John's passionate research into the survival of consciousness after death, some wanted to seek out a professional medium to 'make contact' with John. Others felt such action might be too soon. None of them were aware of John's interactions with me or his readiness to immediately begin communications.

Late that evening, I finally sat down on the sofa. Within seconds, I felt a powerful stream of energy, a lightness, flowing into my head and washing through me. Instinctively, I closed my eyes and crossed my legs into my meditative pose.

With a jerk of intense pain, my right arm contracted into my chest, my body again feeling the impact of John's body against the vehicle—the moment of his passing. It was as if my energy and John's had become overlaid, connected energetically through his right arm. Next, I felt a swift shifting of the energy in my arm, of the emotional debris, the deep shock John must have felt at the moment of the car's impact. I experienced an instant relief to the strong pain.

For some moments I felt my arm spasm, then the pain recede, then a twinge of pain, then relief once more. My thoughts returned to the moment in the shower two days after Shylo's passing, when my consciousness was drawn up and out of my house to meet Shylo. I recalled her reaching down to a fine gold thread, suspended from her body towards me. With a playful smile I saw her tug the gold thread, almost instantly feeling a tug on my umbilicus. I'd grabbed my stomach in surprise, and this brought me rapidly back to being in the shower. Perhaps the heart connections in place with both John and Shylo had enabled the communications between us, had somehow enabled this close connection to take on a new form once they'd passed.

By now it was very late. I sat back and relaxed, stretching to release some of the tension and stiffness. Perhaps John was too busy to visit? Then I felt a slight pain in my upper arm and John walked in. 'Thought I'd find you here,' he said with enthusiasm. 'All's well that ends well.'

'What's well that ends well?' I asked, as he threw his jacket over the chair and sat down on my sofa.

Immediately I was given visions of London and his son Ken's arrival there, to attend to the necessary arrangements. These details would shortly be verified by Maria from Boston. Later, from a higher place of awareness, I would realise that John had been referring to the transformative nature of trauma and tragedy: initially brutal and brittle, but in the end providing an essential opportunity for those involved to transcend the place they had been, and move into the greater expression and experience of their unrealised potential.

John was no longer sitting on my sofa. My room had once again morphed into his house in spirit. Using my psychic vision, I located John in his kitchen on the other side. He seemed to be looking for some morsels to eat. I sat and watched for a short while. Then just as I was about to call out to him, I saw him climb the staircase back towards his bedroom.

Some moments passed and I lost visual contact. Scanning the second level of his home with my interior vision, I found him seated on the sofa in his library, watching TV while he ate. This was typical of John at home in Boston. He was probably watching a Boston Red Sox or Celtics game. There was such a sense of joy and lightness watching him enjoy himself. How different this view of 'heaven' was to the dreary version I'd grown up with! This was so normal, wonderfully ordinary and comforting.

As I looked out his library windows, I noticed it was night. Then suddenly, unexpectedly, it changed to daylight. All the while John sat watching television. No sooner had I questioned why it could be night then day, I received the answer. Just as a television remote can change the stations on TV, in John's new environment he could have the time of day he desired. It was all achieved through thought transference.

'Up here, it's pretty high tech,' said John, still hunched over on the couch, eyes focused on the television. 'Not bad for a retirement place, huh?'

'You haven't changed a bit,' I replied, amused as always by his dry sense of humour.

I was met with an unexpected silence. John had gone. The television was still on and one of the windows was open. I had a strong feeling that something else had drawn his attention, perhaps another part of his house in spirit. I sat for a few moments, warmed by the memory of some wonderful conversations I had had with John in Boston.

Suddenly the warmth of my experience evaporated, leaving behind a haunting sadness and a distinct constriction in my throat. Slowly realising this was someone else's energy and not my own, I felt an uncomfortable sense of foreboding, an eeriness. There was now someone else's unfamiliar energy in the room behind me. As I sat alone in my dimly-lit living room in the middle of a very dark night, I began to feel decidedly intimidated. 'Oh crap!' I suddenly called out, as an intense crawling sensation crept up my back.

By now, I was feeling increasingly ill at ease. The foreboding intensified. The unknown spirit was now standing directly behind me. Remnants of childhood fears crept out from the dark recesses of my memory. I was far from impressed. I knew I had to do something to move past my fear.

With a phrase I'd picked up from a dear English friend, I called out: 'Flipping heck! Who are you?' as I tried to clear the crawling sensation slowly rising up my back.

At that moment, I turned to see the ghostly figure of a young woman with long straight blonde hair, standing very close behind me. 'Okay angels, I need you here now!' I called anxiously. It seemed like the woman's spirit had somehow been drawn into my room, after an interdimensional opening had been created by my interactions with John. I needed help.

Feeling the familiar pain again in my right arm, I stood up and quickly turned on the five ceiling lights in the living room. Gathering confidence, I walked over to the kitchen and turned on the four ceiling lights there too. Now I was no longer in a dimly-lamplit room—it was more like a football stadium on grand final day!

Comforted by the floodlit room, I sat back down at my desk and spoke to John: 'John, what's happening? This is giving me the flipping heebie-jeebies!' The pain in my arm assured me he was still somewhere close by.

From the space just to my left, I noticed a sudden, powerful light. Immediately and intuitively, I began to 'clap' into the energy in front of me, clearing the space around me. With a welcome sense of relief, I saw that one of my guides in spirit had come forward to help, saying: 'You had an uninvited visitor, who noticed your interactions and was drawn into the exchange.'

My hands swung into action once again, clearing and cleansing the space. Intuitively, I was setting up what looked like tall panels of light, walling off the space around the edge of the room. This was sending out a message to all others who were possibly nearby that this space in my home was restricted to John and me, and the divine and sacred guidance of spirit.

My gaze was suddenly drawn to my kitchen. The same woman's ghostly presence was now standing in the far corner of that room, staring across at me. What was she waiting for? What did she need from me? Her sadness and trepidation were tangible.

Feeling more confident from the support I was now receiving from spirit, I spoke to her: 'I want you to feel the love waiting for you beyond the place where you currently live, the place you are holding onto. With great love, I invite you forward into your new life. It is time to let go of the fear of change, the fear of being taken into a whole new life, for it is truly a place filled with love and abundance.'

As I spoke these words, I saw a vivid picture of myself as a young child around four years old. I was swinging on the front gate of my house, dressed in my best winter coat and hat. Within months, I would be a big girl starting school. My hair was in ringlets atop my shoulders. I immediately felt my child-self's insecurity about the imminent change. At that moment, I realised this woman in spirit was also here to be my teacher, to remind me to let go of my fear of the changes about to unfold in my life.

Inspired by this divine understanding flowing through me, I continued to encourage the woman, while absorbing the reassurance for my own emotional child within: 'All you need to do is let go of the fear of what is to come, and simply allow it to happen,' I told her. 'Your life ahead is nothing but light, abundance and love. The one thing left to do now is simply know you are safe, loved and worthy of being in an environment that reflects who you are,' I continued, with a deep knowing and love welling in my heart.

This was a powerful moment for us both. The miracle for me was that it provided insights and wisdom about my own inner emotional debris. This, I was reminded, was the transformative power of the educational and evolutionary nature of life moments. They provide opportunities, however difficult or uncomfortable, for our learning and growth. When we realise this and can connect with this knowing, something inside us is liberated by a greater good.

I felt my spirit guide once more at my side. The woman in spirit was now ready to transition to the other side. I was so touched to see a loving angel standing next to her, ready to escort her into a lighter and more abundant place.

Within moments, the ghostly woman had transitioned. Both she and I had been powerfully liberated. It was then I noticed John standing off to the side, his arms crossed reflectively. He wasn't there alone. A well-dressed man in a suit, shirt and tie was standing with him. It was then I began to hear their discussion of my unfolding spiritual journey, of my life once I moved on from here.

Visions began to appear in my mind's eye. I could see water and a beach, surrounded by beautiful trees. My daughter Jessica and a young man were strolling along the beach, with a child running around near them. Then the perspective suddenly changed. I was there in that very moment in the future. My life felt abundant, fulfilling and expansive. Finally, I could sense the book I'd written and the changes it had brought to my life.

Radiant from the night's deeply moving interactions, I looked over towards John, with gratitude for the enormous healing and growth he was obviously helping create. 'This is just profound, John. This is all just profound,' I slowly began. 'I'm so grateful, John, for all you are doing for me. I can't find words to describe all that I'm feeling right now, with you being here, supporting me in this incredible learning experience.'

Stopping just short of the living room door, I turned round. With my hands on my hips, I playfully added: 'I'll tell you what, John. I'd like to see Spielberg do something with that scene!'

33

CELLULAR MIND

Time seemed to blur, as my nights became my waking hours and mornings my time to sleep. I found myself back at my desk after Jessica and I had enjoyed a beautiful evening of local theatre, and my senses were alerted to John's entrance behind me. I announced to Jessica that I was going downstairs and asked her to call me in an hour.

As I sat on my bed, a cool chill flowed over me. There was a sudden distinct change in the energy of the room. Moments later, I realised John was sitting near me. 'Okay, John. I'm seeing one of my tarot cards, the Sorrow card. And I'm feeling the sadness, the emotion of the many people who feel the enormity of your loss,' I told him.

'It's the way it happened,' he explained. 'That seems to be creating a great deal of grief, anger and emotion, even more than my leaving.'

I took a deep breath, feeling John's serious tone. 'Okay. I'm feeling a constriction in my throat,' I said, 'I'm feeling that bringing about an understanding of the circumstances of your passing seems to be challenging for you.'

For a moment, I was unable to hear John. I tried to tune in as much as I could, but my efforts came to nothing. I just could not pick up what he was trying to say. Frustration was setting in with each passing moment. 'John, I can't seem to hear you as clearly as the other night,' I said, sharing my frustration. 'Is there something you could do, or I could do, to make this flow better?'

Perhaps inferring something more symbolic than literal, John once again reached down to something that looked like an amplifier, adjusted it, then I clearly heard him ask me how it was now. Once again, it was much better. 'Okay, write this down,' John said. 'I left my body straight away. Death is not the end. It's just a passageway, a passing through.'

Immediately, a vision appeared in my mind's eye of the side of a white tent being lifted up momentarily, to allow someone to walk under the flap to the other side. Then a vision appeared of the London subway and the trains there, so I shared what I saw. 'That's right,' John replied. 'Death is a vehicle, not an end.'

I then saw another vision of a television channel momentarily lose transmission, then almost immediately it was restored, as he continued: 'Death is a transference of life energy to a lighter form. We have to be willing to let go of religious dogma, and previously-held scientific doctrine, which we know is limited. We have to readjust our thinking.'

Momentarily, I felt a twinge of pain in my right arm, then a distinct change of energy in the room. I felt another person enter, and the name 'Elisabeth' floated into my mind. 'It was time for him to leave,' the woman said. 'His work is here now with us. We have opened a new centre here, *The Institute to Eradicate Blindness.*

Thoroughly amused by the witty name of John's new centre, I laughed. 'That's very funny! I get it! But why choose me to work with you?'

The woman had shoulder length brown hair. I felt her intelligence and dry humour. She was the same woman I had 'seen' with John the previous day, but it was only then I realised who she was. She had to be Elisabeth Targ, the notable American psychiatrist, whose death and communications from 'the other side' had become the focus of John's research for the last fifteen months. 'We choose to connect with people we know, who have chosen to serve. We also want to honour you for the work you're doing,' she explained.

Then John took over: 'We want the wider health community to know the truth of life beyond death. Things have reached a critical phase. There needs to be a joining of the two streams of knowledge. It is essential that the traditional, medical, psychiatric, scientific way of evaluating the presenting evidence for diagnosis is in collaboration with those who are privy to other ways of evaluating a medical situation that go beyond our known parameters. We need assistance from both sides of the veil—with one supporting the other. Then a whole new and far more exact science can unfold. It will have astonishing scientific results, to change critical thinking around assisting those struggling mental health issues or physical disease. This is no longer an option. We have to break free of old limited understandings and ways of evaluating, to see the effects of a broader nature of reality.'

'We want to find a way to change people's minds, to help them see the value of all there is, all you and others with your sight see,' the woman explained. 'We want to assist people to see the value in changing their perspective, by acknowledging the existence of a different world than the one they know. If we can just establish a way of giving credibility to what people like you see, then there will be a value shift. People will begin to acknowledge that there is value in what you see and know as part of the greater reality. They will also come to know how crucial this wider view is, with respect to the overall methods of clinical evaluation and treatment options available to create enhanced health and wellbeing for their patients.

'It's not an easy task we have ahead of us, as many are unwilling to recognise that anything exists beyond what they can measure with current scientific methods of evaluation. That's why we are coming forward now, why we have been chosen as a group to work together. How we do this, how we successfully bridge this chasm, is still not exactly formulated. We're still very much at the trial and error stage. But with sufficient prayers from our side, people will awaken to the reality of what you already see, what you know to be a wider, more profound understanding of reality.

As this understanding grows, we hope enough people will awaken to the reality of what you see and know to be a true reality, thereby affecting the critical mass necessary to form a new pathway forward for humanity. We hope we can assist in this necessary change, but it is not yet known if we can be successful.'

It was then I heard Jessica call to tell me an hour had passed, though it seemed like much less time to me. Apologising to John and Elisabeth, I joined Jessica upstairs, honouring my agreement with her.

Eventually I returned to my desk, and once again felt a slight pain in my arm. John and Elisabeth were standing by my desk. Moments later, I heard Elisabeth say: 'John, she is as bad as you. She's a workaholic!' Elisabeth's playfulness and humour helped seal the bond I already felt with her. 'You need to rest, to take care of yourself. You need to eat well, keep up your exercise and have enough sleep, as you're going to be very busy,' she continued.

With Jessica now readying for bed, I stood up and began to walk downstairs. 'Thank you so much,' I said halfway down. It was such a relief to relax for the evening.

I climbed into bed gratefully, cosy under my warm doona. Unexpectedly, I felt a gentle shower of energy flow over my head and into my body. 'The cells of the body hold their own layer of cellular consciousness; what I'm talking about here is the mind of each cell,' a man's voice suddenly announced.

Expecting this might turn into a nocturnal tutorial, I rolled over onto my back, in need of pen and paper. I had left them upstairs. 'The cellular mind is connected via telepathic functioning to convey a message of understanding, affecting surrounding cells or other areas in the body,' the voice continued, in a relaxed manner.

By this time, I sensed this was not going to be just a quick few words. 'Hold on a sec!' I interjected, as I leapt out of bed to retrieve my pen and journal.

The tutorial continued: 'Anyone whose vibration is of a high enough frequency can establish communication with the cellular 'mind' of someone else, to enhance, correct or directly affect change in another person's cellular consciousness.

'The power is in being able to access the cellular mind, then bring the cellular mind a new template, a new story. After harnessing the focus of the cellular consciousness, you provide it with a time directive, shifting its focus from the traumas of the past to the present where the trauma no longer exists. It's almost like a teacher passing on instructions to her students, establishing a template, then instilling them with this new information.

'Often, cellular imbalance lies in the past history, stored in the cellular memory. If our cellular consciousness remains stuck in a past traumatic event, like a record needle meeting a scratch or resistance, the same disempowering messages are replayed over and over. Every stuck cellular thought predisposes the physical body of the cell to remain locked in that past condition, predisposing it to weakness, imbalance or pain in that part of the body.

'When the cellular consciousness is burdened by past emotional events and limiting emotional messages, the harnessing of the emotion acts like a cap on the limited script held within the cellular consciousness, trapping the cellular mind, keeping it stuck in what it perceives to be the truth of how things are.

'Working with time is another aspect of creating cellular order. Re-establishing a clear and present script is crucial for maintaining optimum cellular functioning. Bringing cellular awareness to the present moment facilitates detachment to the present time location. Therefore, it is paramount in creating greater understanding of health and healing that new focus is given to treating cellular dysfunction and directly rescripting the limiting life circumstances that have affected cellular health.

'Current methods of dealing with ill-health overlook the import-ance of eradicating the impact of past experiences and previously-loaded perceptions that are held as truth in the cellular mind. There is no need to touch the person's body for these corrections to take place. Firstly, the facilitator accesses the cellular script by way of telepathic thought transfer to uncover the story, to clarify what has been previously recorded or imprinted. Then, the release of the previously-imprinted story is carried out. The facilitator offers the new cellular directive as an energetic and telepathic instruction, to override the old limiting cellular directive. The person's cellular consciousness is then able to operate in the present moment, without being influenced or restricted by past limiting memories that are trapped at the cellular level.

'If the cellular consciousness holds onto the memory of a past injury or limiting circumstance, the cellular consciousness is still experiencing itself as present at the time that previous trauma occurred. So it is still directly affected by that traumatic experience in the past. Cellular rescue, or transfer of cellular placement, restores cellular correctness.

'Often, the cellular consciousness perceives the traumatic event as still occurring, because it has been suspended at that moment of traumatic impact and is still residing in the time frame of that event. The facilitator can restore cellular 'presence' by working with a person's mind, to shed light on the circumstances that led to the traumatic event experienced by the body. While this work takes place in a person's mind, the facilitator can simultaneously read into and influence the person's cellular consciousness. As the person sees how this past trauma is being replayed in their current life, they begin to recognise the limiting patterns that continue to make life circumstances challenging.

'Through retrieval of a cellular memory reliving the past and bringing it through time into present moment, a facilitator can clear the prerecorded cellular story and realign optimum cellular functioning. The patient's mind and cellular mind enter a state of coherence, enabling them to see their lives in sharp focus. Trying to influence the mind, without influencing the cellular mind, will not bring about the same result.'

At this point I apologised, as I couldn't keep my eyes open any longer. I was just too exhausted.

Startled awake again, I saw it was 3am. I sat up in bed and knew I was not alone. I had been awakened from a dream, where I was speaking with John. Scanning the room, I called out to him: 'John! Are you here? You're here, aren't you? Is that you? Flipping ... what's going on? I'm beginning to feel frightened!'

'I'm here,' said John, beside my bed.

My relief was immediate. However, I was still confused. 'Write this down,' John said. 'I need you to connect with Gary Schwartz. Tell him we are going to have a cup of tea and talk about when the battleships are landing on the beach, and when he is going to take a bite out of the apple.'

Struggling to understand the relevance of what seemed to be a ridiculous message, I said: 'John, he's going to think I'm absolutely crazy, if I give him a message like that.'

'Just tell him!' he snapped back. 'I didn't want to keep you up half the night!'

With that John left the room. I was left alone sitting up in the darkness, wondering how I could possibly pass this message to Professor Gary Schwartz who, after receiving his doctorate at Harvard, had become a professor at Yale, then professor of psychiatry, psychology, neurology and surgery at the University of Arizona. I'd never been introduced to him, yet I was to call him with this crazy message. At least he was a well-known researcher and author, focusing his research on the survival of consciousness after death. That offered me some comfort.

It took me ten days, however, to summon the courage to phone him. As I did so, I took a deep calming breath. 'Professor Schwartz, I'm really a very reluctant messenger, because this makes no sense to me. I really need you to know this is not my idea. But I am doing this for Professor Mack, for John. He said to tell you: *We are going to have a cup of tea and talk about when the battleships are landing on the beach and when you are going to take a bite out of the apple.*

'What did you say?' Gary's shock was palpable.

'Look, I'm really sorry Professor Schwartz. I know this sounds really silly ...'

'What phone number did you say you are on? Give it to me and I will call you straight back,' Gary interjected, clearly flummoxed by the message I had shared.

Within seconds, the phone rang and I picked it up. Professor Schwartz was obviously moved by John's message. 'I want to tell you that I have absolutely no doubt that you are in contact with John Mack, and this is why. The message you just passed on to me relates to three separate occasions in my life that I have never shared with anyone else. Not a single person. It refers to three separate incidents that became the three most profoundly-meaningful moments in my life—moments that were turning points for me in knowing that there was something beyond what could be measured or scientifically understood. Your message from John makes reference to each one of those moments.'

34

SOUL HISTORY

The striking confirmation of John's message to Professor Schwartz was powerfully validating for both him and me. The reality of the continuance of life after death made a profound impact on my life. These messages were revealing the truth of our existence beyond death, and what life could be as we fully awaken to our higher human potential.

My consultations continued to be a potent forum for navigating clients to reach their optimal internal elevation and cultivate their greater version and vision of their lives. They also deepened my understanding of health and healing, and the steps required to help the soul evolve.

I walked up the stairs to my office, as usual with little idea as to what would unfold. Those in spirit wanting to assist me with my work were joining us for Anne's session. She was a new client of mine—a beautiful, radiant woman with a gentle nature and long auburn hair.

Anne was an actress. She also had a Reiki healing practice and was involved in other creative endeavours. Hearing about my work from someone in the local community, she'd called me in the hope of a consultation. Ten years ago, Anne had been diagnosed with cancer in her salivary gland. Though some holistic treatments in Mexico had helped, her tumour had recently begun to grow again.

Switching on the tape recorder, I noticed the familiar feelings of love in the room, as those in spirit gathered to assist Anne. 'We always have people in spirit come in,' I explained. 'They always show up to assist. The love they have and their desire to help is unconditional. I've been doing this for many years now, and their loving presence touches me every time.'

As this was Anne's first consultation, I offered reassurance that, even though I worked in a holistic way, I came from a western clinical background. I explained that I wanted to begin by taking some personal medical history.

'Ten years ago, a mass began to appear in my throat,' Anne told me. 'Even as a child, the gland on the right side of my throat was always susceptible. If I had a cold, it would swell. Then ten years ago, a mass began to form in my throat on the right side near my jaw, so my doctor organised for the gland to be removed. Long story short, when the surgeon took the gland out, they found a cancerous tumour. I'd only ever been in hospital to visit someone else at that stage.

'The doctors informed me they wanted to operate and remove part of the floor of my mouth, part of my tongue and all the lymph nodes on the back right side of my throat, then radiate this whole area for six weeks. But I refused. I believed I needed to clear past stagnant emotion that had affected my physical body. I felt this approach could clear it.

'So I've been working over the last ten years to heal this part of my body. I still believe I can heal it naturally. I didn't have radiation before they took the tumour out, and I didn't follow through with any mainstream western medical treatment. At the time, the doctors told me that if I didn't undergo radiation treatment, I would not live beyond three months. But I knew then, as I know now, that I got this for a reason. I know I'm going to discover what that is, and I know when I do it will help others.

'In the ten years since that diagnosis, I have had my mother die and my best friend of 22 years die of breast cancer. I've had a break-up with my family and I've moved from California to Oregon. I also had a lengthy and emotionally-challenging divorce from my husband. It's been a big time for me.'

As I didn't need any further information, the consultation began. 'There is more of the story for you to discover and that is what we're going to find out today,' I assured her. 'I believe we have created this sacred space for you to understand more of your story—your deeper, self-limiting story.'

I then explained that I was moving into my intuitive self, and sensing into her body. 'I'm picking up a lot of sadness, especially around the age of five. It's taking me to a contracted posture that tells me there are feelings of shame in your story, of being unworthy, holding back, holding in, and not being sure of yourself. Does this make sense to you?'

'Yes, uh-huh,' Anne replied, fully engaged in the information she was receiving.

'Okay,' I continued. 'I'm pulling out of that now. I've been taken back to your birth, and there is a feeling of being shut down, shut off. Things are happening quickly. But there's a feeling of having chosen to close down ... So what we are looking at here is the script that you came in with. My attention is being brought to the area between your collarbone and up to just below your nose. Something has been brought in with you, a story located within your cellular memory that I am already picking up on.'

I began to cough quite deeply, as I connected more fully with the emotional debris stored at a cellular level in Anne's jaw area. I then explained what it was I was experiencing: 'That's not me coughing, so much as me responding to the density of the energy trapped in your throat,' I explained. 'So what I can hear, when I tune into this area of your body between your shoulder and just under your nose, is enormous sadness and shame. Also a sense of contraction and unworthiness, a strong desire not to come into earthly form, not to have to go through another life here again. It's almost a feeling of shutting down from what you are to experience in this lifetime. You are aware of the very challenging life script you designed for yourself in this life. This realisation is happening as you're entering your body as a baby. It's resistance to life situations ahead that you are going to have to conquer—basically a lot of emotional pain and challenges, before you get to experience a real breakthrough.

'So let's keep going back in time. We are giving you your story backwards, retracing it backwards. It doesn't always happen this way. Now I'm feeling you very much in a place of light. It's the place you would call home. The place where you come to between incarnations into this physical plane. There is a real feeling of lightness in your body in this place, a great awareness of the bigger picture, of balance and harmony. It's a very beautiful, calm, peaceful feeling. There is a lot of higher understanding available to you here. As a soul, you have attained a great deal of insight, wisdom and knowledge.

'There is a tendency for some people, not you, who choose this level of life challenge in spirit, to think of themselves as being punished when they get here. So they might ask what they have done to deserve this illness or tragic situation. But this is not the truth of the matter. What we are seeing so powerfully is your thinking as a soul, your free will in designing the challenges and learning for your next embodiment here on earth. What you're asking yourself in spirit is: *How best can I bring an understanding to others around me, through my experience in my next embodiment, which will also challenge me and help me grow?*

'So I understand that your current ill health was your request, at a soul level, to achieve certain learning for yourself and others. Those here assisting us from spirit want this to be very clear: that your soul self requested you experience your current health issues. You are the co-creator of your situation.

'It's almost as if your soul self is interested in learning about 'being unwell' and the process of healing, a desire to more fully understand the human condition of ill health. So that is why, in this lifetime, you have been involved in health, healing and wellness, and all the things you can do in a day-to-day sense to heal your body. At the same time, you have literally played out the experience of a 'health crisis' in your life. Does that make sense to you?'

'Yes it does,' Anne replied.

'There was also a necessity for you and your soul group to understand the strong emotions people have, and how they impact on ill health. So as a soul, you actually requested and designed a life here with very powerful moments and days of intense emotion. The tenacity and strength of such intense emotions were unfamiliar to you. That's why it was a very daunting experience to see what lay ahead as you were being born, and why it created some resistance in you.

'I am now being shown what I call your soul book. It's like a thick, sacred, old book. It's in the most amazing place, where all soul books are kept. It's a vast, dimly-lit library. There's a feeling of great sacredness here, as my consciousness hovers over one small area of the books. It's an extraordinary feeling to be aware of all the life experiences of the countless people intricately recorded there. It's like running through a collage of emotions as frequencies that have captured the emotion and experience, be it sadness, grief, joy, sorrow and so on. Everything of consequence in a person's life is symbolically presented to that person as a book, as their soul book.

'What this means is that we are going to access your soul history. My feeling is that there is an important story from the past for you here and now—a story of another lifetime, that will bring you clarity and understanding as to when your cellular story began to manifest as your current ill health. We need to access that story, then clear it on a cellular level, to bring your cellular consciousness back to its original settings and living in the current moment. This is essentially so you stop it replaying the previous limiting incidents. We have to establish 'presence' at your cellular level. Without this, we won't get to the root cause.

'As much as some might want to bombard your tumour with radiation to alter the cancerous cells, what we want today is to bring about a transformation in your mind and cellular mind, by unveiling the hidden emotional story of an experience in your past, and then shift this trapped pain at a cellular consciousness level. So, let's go back and look into the soul book.

'Now, I'm feeling an immediate sensation in my body. The sadness is coming in again very strongly. We are travelling through time to a particular point and place that will give us more of your soul story. I can feel the change in my body, as I enter your past life experience. My attention is being brought to your throat. The person you were then is saying: "I have to keep this quiet. I have to keep this to myself." There is an immediate feeling of secrecy, a feeling that you are involved in a situation that you are choosing to stay silent about. I am being shown a sword pointing downwards. It feels to me that there is some element of danger for you.

'Now I can see you walking along a shoreline, the edge of a lake. I am feeling and seeing you walking along the edge of it. I can see a crystal glass. I feel you have had some alcohol to deaden your pain. There is a decision you have to make, and a lot of emotions around making that decision, great sadness also. I am getting the sense that a house you have come out of has a feeling of great loneliness and sadness for you, a decided lack of love, of being unsupported.'

I paused as the story unfolded around me, watching and waiting for more information, then continued: 'I see. I've just had a vision of what you are intending to do. I'm seeing you taking off an outer garment and leaving it on the shoreline. You're walking slowly into the water. I don't get a very good feeling about this. There is a deep level of sadness within you at that moment ...'

I began to cough heavily again, as I moved closer and closer to Anne's core story, held in the cellular mind of her throat. 'There is someone around you in spirit, as you are taking this action. There has been a lot of confusion in your life. You are reacting to a lot of miscommunication. Someone in spirit, I feel it's an angel to your right, is telling you to go back. I hear him saying: "Go back, it wasn't what you thought!"

'This powerful, yet gentle, angel is with you from moment to moment. He is with you through your thoughts and actions, as you choose what you are going to do. He is giving you unwavering support, constantly holding the possibility of you turning this around. He's gently asking you to go back.

'His presence and instruction are not necessarily going to be heard. Most people receive his message as a feeling, or a sudden questioning of their intention at that moment. You don't realise there is an angel with you, sending these messages and feelings of love, staying with you, holding you in that light space in every moment. The angels look on you as a sacred being, a sacred soul burdened by what you are feeling.

'You are reacting to what has occurred between yourself and your husband. You believe he was having an affair, that he betrayed you with another woman. This has played into your belief of not being good enough, so there's a feeling of great sadness and loneliness.

'I'm getting a sense that your partner was not able to reach you, as you were locked into your dungeon of emotions around this situation. You had really pulled away from him and become very serious, sombre and reflective. Yet when you met, you had such liveliness. Your husband loved that you were so alive! But at some point, your lack of belief in yourself began to consume you, so you believed he loved someone else.

'Your husband needed to be looked after and loved. You weren't able to give him this love and support, because you were sad and felt isolated. He had a soul connection with this other woman, who seems to have dark hair. Yet I don't believe anything physically happened. You thought it did, and that despair pushed you into wanting to end your life.

'So let's continue. I'm being brought back once again to your throat, to the moment you made the choice to wade further into the water. For some reason the angel has stopped sending you messages and is just being with you. He has ceased his attempts to influence you. It's such a powerful and devastating moment. Yet it's such a deeply-loving feeling from this angel. This is so tragic, yet so beautiful and touching. The angel has realised you have passed the point where he can influence your choice. So instead, he is holding you in the most divine love, gently encircling your soul with his love. It is the most exquisite feeling, yet so sad. You chose at that point to pass from that lifetime, and I see you very gently go under the water. It is night. The water is dark and still.

'So I am going into your cellular consciousness now in that moment, and you are saying: "Don't take me back there, I don't want to go back there. I don't want to feel dishonoured. This feeling is too overwhelming. I have come to the point of understanding, and I wish to be released."

'I hear another person's voice. This person is very unconditional, very wise, very honouring, and he is saying: "This request can be granted to you, but you must understand that you will have to return again later, in order to complete the learning." Your request is granted and you are then welcomed with great love back into 'creation.' There's a lot of relief for you, and you feel greatly honoured as you return home.

'So, more significant than these details of your life story, those in spirit are calling your attention to the level of despair and sadness you felt then, and your experience of betrayal. With this event came the longing to be loved, the searching for love, the need to feel loved, and the theme of betrayal. These are the really significant elements they want to highlight for you.

'What happened is that your throat stored the cellular memory of this experience. I'm feeling that again in the jaw, through the throat and up into the mouth. So this is the area in your body where this limiting old cellular script has affected your health and cellular function. It has created the imbalance. As you couldn't share your pain, you remained silent. You kept your feelings as a secret locked in your throat.

'In choosing to end that life, you had to agree to return at a later point, to take up the same challenges once more and create an opportunity to overcome them. Going forward, the higher life script for you to live by is to accept that you are worthy of love, and that you are so complete already.

'The first healing step has been to show you this limiting story from your past. A shift in your cellular consciousness has already been triggered on accessing this story, with the learning and deeper understanding it brings.

'Okay, I'm being brought back to this current time. I'm seeing a vision of rushing through a time tunnel, like a wormhole or time corridor that has a 'rushing back' feeling. I'm just waiting, as my energy doesn't seem quite fully back yet.

'Oh ... the reason that I am being held back from fully returning is that there's another piece of information for you from that same past life experience. There was a woman in that lifetime who was motherly to you. She wasn't necessarily your mother, but she loved you a great deal. She didn't live where you lived, she lived further away. There was a great deal of despair when she heard the actions you'd taken. As a soul, when you realised later what that did to her, you wanted to support her when you came back here again. This woman has been very close to you in your current life, very caring, very present in her conversations and interaction with you. She has lighter hair and is a great listener and very loving. Does someone come up for you as I describe this to you?'

'Is this person still alive?' Anne inquired.

'I'm getting a sense you knew this person in California, and you shared so much time together.'

'It's Rebecca, I'm sure,' said Anne.

'Oh okay. Is this the lady with breast cancer, who you said passed over?'

'Yes,' she said, slowly nodding her head.

'She had quite a sense of humour, and there was lots of laughter together. Does that make sense?'

'It does,' said Anne smiling.

'Okay. Those in spirit just wanted you to know Rebecca was the woman I was mentioning, who you knew in that previous lifetime. She came back again in this lifetime to be with you, so she could support you. As a soul, she desired to support you in that other lifetime but that desire wasn't fulfilled. Was she around you when you were younger, and when your children were quite young?'

Anne nodded.

'Yeah, that's what she is telling me. She is here now. I'm seeing her picking the kids up in the morning and saying she will see you again later that day. You seemed to see a lot of each other. That's really special. Why is she showing me fruit? There is something about fruit ... Oh, I see. She's saying to me that you have tried all sorts of things, from a healthy diet to herbal supplements, and you've been to a lot of places to try to regain your health and wellness.

'She's relieved you have come here today. There is a real sense of relief. She said this is going to be significant. She cares so much about you,' I said, as I looked into Anne's eyes, now filling with tears.

'How do you feel, knowing she is here?' I asked.

'It's so special. I love her so much,' Anne replied, tears now flowing down her face.

'I can feel that too. It is so special she is here, and that she loves you too. She loves you absolutely,' I continued.

It was then that Anne made a significant disclosure. 'Rebecca was afraid I was going to end my life, years ago before she died. I was so down and depressed with the tumour and my divorce,' Anne revealed.

'It must have been a really difficult time,' I replied. 'So you must have related so much with the lifetime I just described to you.'

'Totally. Everything you said made so much sense and relates so much to my life now,' Anne confirmed. Her relief was tangible.

'Okay. So now we need to honour your friend Rebecca's script, her involvement with you in that past life, then honour her presence in your current life and now, as she interacts with you from spirit. The connection between you is so significant. She is a very loving, strong presence around you, really committed to supporting you.

'That's a really good piece of your puzzle, because I am being shown there are times when you feel very much alone. Those in spirit want you to completely get that we are never alone. It's just an illusion. We are truly never alone. There are times when we go through great learning. Others around us in spirit may pull back, to allow us to really experience what we are meant to experience. But they haven't disappeared. They are just further back, because of the intensity of emotion we are experiencing at the time.

'The wise ones in spirit want you to understand you are not alone in the experience you're going through now either. Your current difficult feelings come from your experience in that past life, where you felt very alone and full of despair.

'What we are doing now is removing the old programs, the old cellular script. Now that you understand how you have held onto this painful story, you have already lessened its intensity and impact.

'What we do now is instruct the cellular memory to align with higher, healthier frequencies and cease resonating within that painful, low-frequency story. It's like installing a new software program that enables your computer to be more effective, more attuned to your current needs. We are going to go straight into this. I don't need to come any closer or touch you. We are preparing the cellular consciousness for change.'

With my right arm extended and my index finger pointing out, I psychically placed my finger right in the middle of Anne's head. As I did so, I saw a point of light radiating down through her cellular body. I began to cough once again, as we moved that light down into Anne's throat.

'We are infiltrating the denser cellular structure in your jaw and throat area, working directly with that. My arm is like a laser beam, bringing high-frequency light and information into the cells there. These cells are effectively being given a new operational directive; being educated to understand they are no longer required to fulfil your old story. We are inviting the cellular consciousness to change.

'I am just going to stand closer to you. We are now decommissioning the old unhelpful script of this particular mass here in your jaw. It is very heavy, like picking up huge pieces of firewood, very heavy ... and I am passing it into spirit where it will change its form. I am seeing that heavy energy going into a tunnel of very bright light and being transformed into light. Can you feel that? There is such a feeling of love here now,' I explained, bursting into joyful laughter.

'Thank you universe; this is just so precious and beautiful. Feel that love flowing into you. We invite you to embrace that love and bring it into every cell of your body. Isn't the feeling extraordinary? Can you feel the intensity and power of that?' I asked Anne, my eyes flooding with tears. 'I am being asked to say that this is the universe's version of treating your tumour. Western medicine's answer is to blast your tumour with a really dense vibration of radiation, whereas what we are doing here is the opposite. We are bringing into your tumour an incredibly high vibration of love, so every cell is aligned with this new understanding.'

I continued the energy treatment, clearing Anne's right hip area. Looking psychically into her body, she looked wonderful. Her energy was radiant with light. When I asked what she was feeling, Anne said she felt very grateful, altered, like she had just had surgery on some level. She could feel something happening in her throat.

'You know, I have felt sad ever since I was born really,' Anne commented. 'My husband left and that was very devastating. I always wanted a partner. I wanted to feel pretty since I was a small child, always wanted to be needed. So the past eight years of not being in a relationship and then my last child going off to college have been really challenging, even though I have known that my soul self really needed to be alone, to have that experience. The fear I seemed to have all my life was that there was something wrong with me, and because of that I wouldn't be loved, I wouldn't be enough.'

'The most destructive malaise in society is shame,' I echoed. 'Not believing in ourselves—that we are of value, that we are worthy, that we are enough.'

I felt such regard for this beautiful soul, for her learning and growth, and for the awakening of others who would be touched by her story. 'Love can move mountains,' I said, as I stood up and walked over to give her a hug. It was time to say goodbye. Anne was leaving to drive to Seattle in the morning.

Having finished for the day, I rode off slowly down the street on my bicycle, overwhelmed by the beauty of autumn around me. I felt a profound sense of blessing, having experienced all I'd been privileged to see during the last two hours. Like the leaves on the trees that flagged my path, I bathed in the glow of the afternoon sun, and was reminded that life here on this beautiful planet is incredibly precious.

35

AN UNEXPECTED
ARRIVAL

Extraordinary events continued to consume my every waking hour, and would creep not so quietly into my attempts to sleep. After Shylo and then John's unexpected communications from the other side, I realised I was not in control of where this ride was taking me. At times I would find myself entertaining romantic notions. Would I meet someone special? Would I finally be able to create a stable home for Jessica? Would I be offered some significant career opportunity? These fragrant thoughts fortified me as I woke each morning, stemming from my hope that despite these devastating traumas, something good, and perhaps great, would rise up from the ashes to transcend and transform other lives.

A few days later, I sat alone at my desk. Suddenly, one of my daughter's friends popped up via MSN message on my computer screen. This wasn't unexpected, as I'd often enjoyed spontaneous chats with Jessica's old schoolfriends in Australia. The message was from Justine: *I'm so sad because ...* The rest of the message drove a stake into my heart, as I struggled to comprehend what I was reading: *Mia tried to commit suicide. They took her off the respirator today. She is going to die.* Shocked and terrified, I found it enormously difficult to breathe.

Mia had been Jessica's close friend for many years, and had remained close since our move to North America. She'd been planning to visit the US. She and Jessica had their hearts set on a trip to Disneyland and New York. Not death, I couldn't take another death. Mia couldn't die.

I quickly sent a reply back, asking what had happened and for Justine's phone number so I could call her, but got no reply. 'No!' I screamed to the empty room. I wouldn't allow Mia to die. She was only fourteen. Hurrying to the phone, I called Jessica's father in Australia.

'Mark, it's me,' I began, trying not to wake Jessica downstairs. The reception was bad and my emotional state didn't help.

'What's going on, Liz?' he asked.

I explained what I'd just been told and how devastated I felt, and asked if he knew any further details.

'Just be very careful what you say and who you say it to,' he cautioned. 'You don't even know if this is true.'

'I know it's true. I know it in my soul. I'm going to call one of the other mums from school. I need to know what happened and how Mia is. There may be something I can do,' I said, ending the call.

With trembling hands, I pulled out my phone book, searching for one of the mothers whose daughter had also been a close friend of Mia. The shock in Katherine's voice indicated she hadn't heard anything. She'd last seen Mia three days before, looking wet and cold as she walked home in the rain. Katherine had stopped and offered her a lift, but Mia had refused, wanting to walk home alone. That had been early on Monday afternoon. By midafternoon that same day, she'd tried to end her life.

'If only I'd forced her to get in the car, maybe she wouldn't have done what she did,' cried Katherine. I hung up the phone, leaving Katherine to try to find out what was happening.

It was now 2.30am. Praying I could do something, I buried my face in my hands, feeling utterly powerless. Then suddenly, I felt a calming light flow over me. At that moment, a part of me left my body. I was suddenly in Mia's hospital room. I recognised it straightaway. She was in one of the main teaching hospitals in Sydney, where I'd previously worked. Intuitively I raised my arms, sending her energy and love, pleading with the universe for me to help heal her.

After a few moments, I was slowly drawn forward by an unseen force. The next moment I was reaching for Mia's face, for her head. My hand momentarily touched her forehead. I was instantly struck by a feeling of impending death. Her brain had been severely damaged. I suddenly knew she'd never recover. Mia no longer felt alive. I recoiled in horror.

The strength in my legs gave way, as I fell forward onto my knees, sobbing. As I sobbed, a sudden knowing emerged from within. The same knowing that I'd felt when I received the calls about Shylo's devastating suicide and John's unexpected death. A deep knowing that there was some level of higher purpose to this circumstance that would help awaken many.

Right now, however, I rejected this knowing, fully determined to do everything within my power to bring Mia back to life. Pushing myself up from the floor, I walked across to the kitchen, picked up the phone and called the hospital in Sydney. Within moments, it was confirmed that Mia was there in a critical condition.

Within moments I was put through to the ward and spoke unexpectedly to her aunt. 'What do you need to know? I'm not sure how much you are aware of?' she began, her voice vulnerable. I attempted a response. She in turn offered a brief explanation: 'Mia has been taken off the respirator and is breathing on her own. The doctors have told us she has suffered extensive brain damage, and they know she won't live.'

'Would you just do one thing for me?' I asked. 'Would you go to Mia and give her my love? Would you tell her Jessica and I love her and miss her? Could you kiss her little hand for us, to let her know we are there with her?'

'I will, I will,' came her gentle reply.

Ending the call, I felt completely bereft. My thoughts were now with Jessica who lay asleep downstairs.

What Mia had done suddenly seemed unimaginable. Knowing that Jessica had just lost her close friend was too much to even contemplate. I picked up the phone and called my sister, Sandra. Though we had not spoken more than three times in the past twelve months, I needed her support.

'I'm sorry Liz, that's awful. You must feel really overwhelmed,' she began kindly. 'But you can't blame yourself. You couldn't have done any more than you did.'

'I don't want her to die. I don't want any of them to die. They are such beautiful children, and I care about them so much. First it was Shylo and now Mia. John's death was only two weeks ago. I didn't want any of them to die!'

We spoke for about twenty minutes. By the time I ended the call, it was almost 4am. I switched off the lights in the living room and walked downstairs, exhausted and deeply sad. I tiptoed into Jessica's room and kissed her head, wanting desperately to shield her from the pain she would feel in the next few hours.

I tried to sleep but couldn't, so I made several more calls to Australia. By 5.30am I was finally asleep, only to be woken up by Jessica standing by my bed, worried she was late for school. She knew there was something wrong. I could hear it in her voice as she tried to wake me.

We sat and cried on the bed together, as Jessica struggled to take in the tragic news. She kept asking me why Mia would take her own life. Several hours later, after a comforting hot chocolate at a nearby cafe, we visited Jessica's school to inform the teachers what had happened and to tell them she wouldn't be at school for a while.

When we arrived home Jessica sat on the sofa watching television, while I sat at my desk and opened up one of the documents I'd been working on. Suddenly a powerful energy descended. My body was turned around on my chair and I was drawn into the middle of the room. Spontaneously, I was taken into a corridor in Mia's hospital. I could clearly see Mia standing in the shadows of the corridor. I knew straightaway that her physical body had stopped breathing. Yet she was still waiting there in spirit in the hospital corridor.

The very next moment a psychic connection surged from me to Mia. At the moment we connected, I knew what had to be done: 'Mia, I'm going to help you sweetheart,' I explained.

I could see a huge shaft of light pour out through me into her chest. The light expanded, as if to draw her into it. Next, a beautiful tall angel stepped through the light and into the corridor where Mia stood. As the shaft of light opened up even further around Mia, I witnessed an incredible spectacle. The very next moment I saw many people surrounding Mia, welcoming her home into the light. She had transitioned. I watched spellbound, as an older male relative lovingly stepped forward to embrace her.

Then, just as suddenly, I was back in our living room in southern Oregon. I calculated it was very early in the morning in Australia. Walking over to Jessica on the couch, I wrapped my arms around her and gently told her: 'I think Mia's stopped breathing now, sweetheart. I think she's gone now.'

Later that evening I called Mia's father, Michael, to offer support. He confirmed that Mia had passed away in the night, just prior to the time I had been psychically taken to assist in her transition. Restraining my own grief, I listened as Michael spoke of Mia's struggle with her intense sadness. I'd no idea her emotional state had deteriorated so far. I felt such despair at not having been able to be more involved. Once again, my choice to leave Australia weighed heavily on my mind.

Michael then explained he'd had a feeling of foreboding the entire day of Mia's suicide. As a doctor, he was in his clinic that fateful afternoon. He said that at the exact time of Mia's suicide, his right arm had shaken uncontrollably, and he'd been overtaken by an intense feeling of dread. He also told me he had taken to reading the Bible over the past eighteen months, to somehow try and make sense of his life, and what was happening with Mia. She had been seeing a psychiatrist, who had prescribed antidepressants. In hindsight, Michael questioned whether the antidepressant could have caused her to take her life, as suicidal thoughts were possible side effects.

His next comment touched my heart. 'Mia really loved you, I know that. She spoke a lot about you and Jess, and felt very close to both of you. She always called you Mum, and I know you meant a lot to her.' I took comfort in the fact that Mia and several other girls at school had taken to calling me 'Mum' in the final year before we left.

Reluctantly ending the call, I asked him to stay in touch, and to let us know the details of her funeral. The rest of the evening seemed to pass in a haze of sadness. About 1am, I finally made it to bed. Pulling my doona up close to my face I spoke to Mia, sending her our love and asking the angels to be with her. It was at that point I suddenly heard the voice of a little girl calling out to me: 'Mia's here! Mia's here!'

Opening my eyes, I noticed the hall light gently shining into my room, then heard Mia timidly ask: 'I've never done this before, so am I meant to talk to you, or do you ask me things?' She was sitting on my bed next to me, her back against my French antique bedhead, her legs curled around beside her.

'Oh, sweetheart!' I exclaimed, melting into tears. Then I felt an intense pressure on my throat and began to choke and cough. Struggling, I pulled myself back from the intensity of the experience. 'Can you tell me what happened when you left, sweetie?' I gently asked.

'I kind of heard voices, like distant voices, like if kids were across the road ... muffled. I couldn't clearly hear them. Then I felt like cool air, like floating, lifting ... Then it was all dark, and I couldn't see where I was. I'd gotten stuck ... make that I got stuck getting out, because I didn't know if I was going to stay or not. That's when you helped me. I told Mum I hated her. I hated what she did, not what she was. I couldn't get through to her. I couldn't make her understand.'

At that point, I noticed the taste of smoke, like cigarette smoke in my mouth. 'Did you smoke, Mia?' I asked, surprised.

'Sometimes,' came her soft reply. 'I'm so glad you can hear me,' she continued, her voice sounding warm and comforted. 'Can you see me?' she asked.

Using my psychic vision, I looked once again. I could clearly see her sitting next to me on my bed. 'In my mind's eye,' I replied, aware of the poignancy of the moment. 'I know it was painful for you, but do you have a message for your mum or your dad, or your brother or sister?'

I could feel Mia's mood shift, as she responded to my question: 'I won't hurt her anymore ... no more fights, no more arguing, no more yelling, no more screaming,' her voice was now slow, reflective. She stood up from the bed. 'They want me to leave now. I need to adjust to all this,' she said, as she began to turn and walk away.

'Do you have a message for Jessica?' I asked, longing to continue our conversation.

Mia turned her head towards me, paused then replied: 'Tell her I wouldn't recommend what I did.'

As she left, I looked at my bedside clock. Thirty minutes had passed since the child's voice first heralded Mia's arrival, though it seemed like only ten minutes.

Immediately, I began to feel someone moving about in spirit next to my bed. The very next moment I clearly saw John and heard him say: 'It's very sad, very sad. She's going to feel better because of her communication with you. It's going to make her feel better.'

'They knew,' he continued. 'Those in spirit around her knew this was coming for some time, and they were ready. They would talk with her in her sleep, trying to straightening out her wires, adjusting her perceptions of how she believed things were. In the end, it didn't matter.'

'When you say it didn't matter, John, what do you mean exactly?' I asked.

'They knew their efforts weren't going to come to anything. It became too big a task for them to effectively intervene. By that stage, they had to step back,' he replied.

At that moment, I looked over to my doorway and noticed a light. Someone else was standing in spirit near my door. As I looked, the light became clearer, then I was immediately drawn back to my conversation with John: 'She's okay here now,' he told me. 'They're looking after her. She's adjusting, taking it gently.'

I was overwhelmed with tiredness and a sensation of slowing right down. I could still feel a slight tightness around my throat as John continued: 'They just medicate,' he said, referring to the mainstream medical profession. 'That's all they know. That's the way they treat situations like this. They need to understand that what they're doing is so limited. There are so many other areas of inquiry to bring real understanding and insight into a situation like this, so many different methods of correcting the imbalance. We're going to make them stand up on their toes!'

With that, John left. As he did so, the whole room altered energetically. Another thirty minutes had passed. Propped up against my pillow, I was feeling overwhelmed, yet deeply grateful for these insights.

At lunchtime the following day I was holding Jessica next to me on the sofa, as we talked and cried about Mia's death. Jessica was devastated with the double tragedy of John being killed in London only two weeks earlier, and now Mia ending her life.

'But she didn't even call me! She promised that if things got really bad for her, she would call me,' Jessica sobbed.

'I know, I know,' I said, holding her in my arms.

'We made a promise before I left school,' continued Jessica tearfully. 'It was a pinkie promise. She was supposed to call. And I was supposed to be there for her. But she never did.'

Powerlessness overwhelmed me. There just seemed to be so little I could do to lessen the intensity of Jessica's pain. At that moment, I noticed the energy in the room change. As I looked across the room, I tried to tune in to who was 'coming in.' It was Mia, slowly walking towards the armchair in front of us. Her approach was apprehensive. She was clearly aware of Jessica's intense emotion and unsure how her presence was going to be received.

'I think Mia's here, Jessie,' I gently explained, as I looked across to the armchair.

'But she's **not** here!' said Jessica, through huge sobs.

'But she is here,' I softly replied. It was then that the communication began: 'Mia is saying she wants you to know she is not in pain anymore. She wants you to know that it's like she had a big tummy pain for so long, and now it's gone,' I gently explained.

'Yeah, but now I have a big tummy pain,' Jessica replied, still crying.

'She's saying that she wants you to do all the things that she didn't get to do, because it will be like she is doing them. She's showing me that she is going to come and watch you dance today, at your dance practice at school this afternoon, Jessie. She's been offered these times to come to visit me and to see you, but she can only stay a little while. It's just short visits right now. She's leaving again. She's waving and saying goodbye.'

At that point, I saw Mia walk away from us. Looking back at Jessica I clearly heard her softly say: 'Bye! Bye. Jess!'

Two hours later, Jessica felt strong enough to attend her dance team practice. They were in training for a football match the following week. As I sat on my own in the bleachers, I noticed a distinct energy shift once again. There to my right was Mia. She seemed like anyone would after a powerful trauma: vulnerable and adjusting to a new awareness.

Looking back to the football field, forty exuberant children from eight to eighteen were dancing and talking and practising their routines. I wondered how it was for Mia, now that she was coming to terms with life here on earth progressing without her. She would have loved to have been here with Jessica at an American school, with boys, gridiron games and cheerleading.

Suddenly, all the girls walked off the field to practise their entry again. I felt Mia's energy even more intensely. Glancing around behind me, I could see her sitting to my left now, one row higher than mine.

She smiled and looked at the girls as they danced onto the field. As she smiled, I was reminded of how beautiful she was. Seeing her here, my heart went out to her. How painfully real the consequences of her actions must be to her right now.

Yet already there was more of an ease about her. She seemed more accepting of being where she was and seeing life from her new reality. At that moment, I realised that just as we here have to adjust and grieve and heal our emotions after the loss of someone we love, so too do those who pass over. They also have to go through a period of adjustment, of closure from the life they've just had.

It was clear that Mia was being assisted in her adjustment by being able to visit with me, to communicate and be heard. Being seen and understood by someone she knew and felt close to this side of the veil seemed hugely beneficial. I hoped that in time her life, her passing and communications from the spirit world would bring the same level of healing and support to many others.

Strains of Michael Jackson's *Thriller* boomed from the football field. It brought me back to the moment, to the joy of life. I searched for Jessica among the streamers and high kicks, and caught sight of her next to her friend, Stephanie. At that moment, her preciousness to me was beyond words.

TRAGEDY BRINGS TRANSFORMATION

At just fourteen, Jessica was about to fly back to Australia to attend Mia's funeral. Jessica was to fly back alone, as I couldn't afford to travel back with her. This just made the whole situation even more painful and poignant. Jessica was suffering intensely. I felt such guilt about taking her away from Mia and her old school, and found myself raking over my past, just as I had done after her father's accident in the outback.

Downstairs, Jessica was packing for her trip. Standing in her doorway, I longed to help my beautiful daughter, but what could I say? How could I reach her? 'I can't imagine how sad and unreal it must be to be packing to go back for Mia's funeral,' I said, breaking the silence.

'She didn't think of that though, did she?' Jessica replied. 'She didn't think of that when she did what she did. She didn't think about how hard it would be for us to think of what she did, to know that she won't be coming back, to have to live our lives without her!'

'I'm sure she didn't even know what to think in the end, darling,' I replied, trying to offer some level of understanding.

Suddenly, that same little voice in spirit chimed in: 'Mia's here! Mia's here!' I realised Mia was standing on the left-hand side of Jessica's bed. Within moments, she began to speak. 'I know I didn't call. I didn't see it at the time. It was like I was clouded by a dust storm. I couldn't see what was outside of that. My friends, my family ... just the pieces of dust.'

'I don't know what to wear to the funeral,' Jessica interjected, full of anger and pain.

'Mia wants to help you choose something to wear, sweetheart,' I gently shared.

'I don't care!' Jessica replied.

'Jessica is really hurting right now, Mia,' I explained, trying to facilitate the communication, yet knowing how much of a struggle it was for all of us.

Mia looked across at me and said: 'I don't know what to say about her hurting. I just don't know what to say.' She looked towards Jessica and gently continued: 'There are animals here in spirit ... I like the chequered socks you have that go above your knee.'

'So do I,' said Jessica coldly, as I shared with her Mia's reply.

'I'm learning lots of things here, and the teachers are really nice. Not like our school,' Mia shared timidly.

This time Mia's comments were met with silence from Jessica. It was so challenging for her and there was only so much Jessica could take. It was a fine line I was treading. Placing my trust in the divine order of things, I continued to talk with Mia, sharing her comments and responses with Jessica as gently as I could.

'Mia, what are you learning there, where you are now?' I asked, making myself comfortable on Jessica's bedroom floor.

'That life's like a game. That you get to choose the moves and that creates your way forward. I fucked up,' she said, moving to sit by me on the floor.

'What do you mean, honey?' I replied.

'I didn't listen. I didn't want to listen,' she explained.

After that comment, Jessica walked out of the room and into her bathroom, shutting the door. I didn't blame her. She was angry. Mia and I both understood that.

After a few moments, I spoke to Mia again: 'We both love you and are here for you. Jessie is having such a hard time with you leaving, but how can I help? Is there anything I can do to help you right now, sweetheart?'

'It's really nice to talk with you. Just to have you listen. That's really nice,' she replied.

At that moment, Jessica walked in again. Turning, I stood up and spoke to her: 'Jessie, I know this is all so hard and painful for you.'

'Yes it's hard!' she angrily replied. 'She killed herself. I'm angry about that. That's hard,' she continued, her eyes flooding with tears.

'I know, honey. It hurts me too; but Mia is coming to speak to you for a reason. She is trying to help you. She wants you to know that she cares about you, and that you are still friends, even though she is over there now.'

Once again, Jessica left the room.

'It's just as difficult on this side for us you know,' Mia continued. 'Usually no-one much on your side can see or hear us. So it's just as hard for us to adjust as it is for you, when you don't see or hear us anymore.'

I suddenly realised that leaving this life behind required a significant process of adjustment, support, compassion and understanding—the same as it did for those who remained. My moment of reflection was interrupted, as Jessica silently re-entered the room and continued to pack. As she tucked her toiletries into her suitcase, I heard Mia softly say goodbye.

No sooner had she gone than my right arm and wrist began to hurt. It was then I heard John's voice: 'We need to provide more detail about what it's like here. It's still too abstract. People need to know what it's like here ... more tangible details would be useful. That would make it easier for people to connect with us. The language and experience of life beyond death means we are really re-educating people to a whole new way of understanding life here in this plane, and beyond. It's like acclimatising to a whole new place.'

After writing down his message, I walked upstairs to find Jessica looking for pictures of Mia to take back to Australia. Walking slowly up behind her, I wrapped my arms around her: 'I really understand that you're angry. It's normal to feel that way. I want you to know that I'm here for you. I get such a strong knowing that Mia is coming to talk to you, so you can both grow and learn and move forward together.

'And even though I see and sense more than most people, it doesn't mean I don't feel any pain. I am hurting so much because she did what she did. I hurt that you have to live a life without her here. I know you are angry about her choice to leave, but I'm here loving and holding you, just as I've always done. That will never change.'

As it happened, bad weather prevented Jessica from being able to fly out the following day. As we arrived back from the airport, I was relieved her plane had been delayed.

Later that evening, Mia suddenly appeared. 'No more schoolwork, no more books, no more teachers' dirty looks!' she exclaimed, in a gentle playful chant. Sharing this message with Jessica brought a smile, the first in days, thawing her sadness and anger. Jessica told me that at the end of every school year, her group of friends, Mia included, would call this out to each other as they gathered together at the end of the final day.

So Mia had found a way to capture Jessica's heart after all, to nudge it beyond its darkness of grief with something normal and known.

With a lightness of heart, I continued to share Mia's chatter. 'Mia is showing me what looks like long, thin, metal poles that somehow make music. They look to be outside at school somewhere. Do you know what these are, Jessie?'

Again Jessica's face lit up with amusement. 'Yeah! We used to eat lunch near them. They were bells. We used to play games around them, and sometimes we would shake them violently, so they would make crazy noises ... it was so hilarious!'

'Okay. So now I'm seeing these huge cookies. Mia is showing me these huge cookies. Does this make sense to you, darling?'

'We used to eat those at lunchtime,' Jessica replied, more relaxed. 'I used to go down and buy the girls cookies at lunch, because Mia and some others wouldn't eat anything for lunch sometimes. I knew if I bought them cookies, they'd eat them. They were chocolate chip cookies that were half dipped in chocolate. They were like some of the best cookies I've ever had in my life!' continued Jessica, her face softening with each reply. 'Does she remember the mafia voice? She used to do the mafia voice. It was so funny!'

Within seconds, I could feel my face taking on a playful expression shaped by Mia's thoughts. Jessica sat mesmerised, watching my face move. Some seconds later she exclaimed: 'That's it! That's how she did it!' She was in no doubt now of Mia's presence.

'I didn't like it at our school, but I like it here,' Mia continued. 'We're learning lots of different things. At first it's like they show you a movie of your life, and they stop at times and show you what happened at that stage, to lead to something else happening. It's like they join the dots, help you make sense of where you could have made other choices, or done other things that would have affected your life and your life experiences more positively. They call it Life Mapping.'

As Jessica continued to chat about their old school antics, we were interrupted by a distinct shift in the room's energy as Shylo walked in.

'Looks like you're getting the bigger picture now!' she said enthusiastically. 'You can have the environment here how you really want it to be, for the experience you want to have. It's like you re-experience a particular memory to understand it more. There's no struggle to leave the classroom. You don't want to get away from the teaching, because the teaching is different. It's learning about different levels of things ... character building, life planning, things like that,' she continued, standing next to Jessica, who was sitting in the armchair.

'So do you have non-radioactive food in the cafeterias there?' Jessica responded playfully. Many of her American school friends complained about the food available at the school cafeteria, often referring to it as radioactive.

'You can have whatever food you want to experience,' said Shylo. 'You don't need food to nourish you, but people can have the choice to eat any food they want.'

'I have Coca-Cola!' chimed Mia.

'Mia's saying she has Coca-Cola, Jessie. Did she like that drink then?' I asked, surprised.

'Yeah, she did,' Jessica replied.

Inspired, I opened my laptop and began to journal these communications. As I was writing, I suddenly received the feeling that the girls were being called back to creation. Glancing up at the clock, I was surprised to find it was almost midnight.

Turning back to Jessica, I saw Shylo crouched down beside her, as if ready to share something with her. 'Shylo is showing me a horse paddock. There's a fence all the way around, with some horses in the middle. She's saying that this is like life. You climb over the fence and onto a horse. You ride around for a while until it's your turn to get off, then you climb over the fence again. She's saying that once you're over the other side of the fence, you know that both inside and outside of the fence exists.'

Then Shylo pointed to Mia and said to Jessica: 'You need to listen to her. She is going to teach you a lot.' At that point, she stood ready to leave. 'I hope you have a good flight back,' she said to Jessica, then began to walk back towards the hallway. Almost immediately, Mia moved quickly past Jessica, through the kitchen and was gone.

Later as I lay in bed, I suddenly noticed a soft light glow. Within seconds, the glow became a radiant doorway of light and I began to experience a beautiful feeling of love and lightness from within the light flowing over me. In what seemed liked seconds, a most loving older woman in her sixties emerged from within the glow of exquisite light. She had soft grey hair tied in a loose bun and had an expression of absolute kindness on her face. As she gazed at me, her eyes connected deep within my soul. 'We want to thank you for the support you are giving to Mia,' she said. 'She is being assisted greatly by being able to communicate with you. She knows you can see her and hear her, and that is making a significant difference to her. Because of that, it is assisting her progress and adjustment to being here. Rest now. We bring you much love.'

The next thing I knew it was morning. The sunlight had found its way through my curtains. I rose late and walked upstairs. As I passed the front door, peering in at me was a huge wild turkey—the first I had ever seen. I knew straightaway there was a higher reason for its appearance. Finding my Animal Medicine Card Set, I looked up the symbolic meaning of turkey: *Simply stated, it is the deep and abiding recognition of the sacrifices of both self and others ... in turkey's death, we have our life.* Deeply moved, I was drawn back to the front door and stood silently staring out at the grand bird.

Had these beautiful teenagers died so that many others could learn, in the aftermath of their death, about the soul's progression beyond death? That thought stayed with me.

A few minutes later, as I sat at the kitchen bench opening my emails, I felt it important to write to Mia's father and share more detail about her visits. The idea seemed to bring with it a sense of radiance, so I knew it was divinely inspired.

As I sat writing to him, Mia suddenly appeared: 'I want to talk to my mum!'

Chills rolled over me, as I sensed the intensity of her request. Mia's mother wasn't going to be open to Mia's visitations in spirit, I knew that. So I chose instead to send the message to Mia's father, as part of the email I'd just begun. Then I sat and listened as Mia continued: 'I'm sorry I said the things that I said. I'm sorry Mum had to find me like she did. I don't blame her. I don't hold anything against her. I just want her to let go of thinking it was her fault. It's no-one's fault. It's the choice I made. I really didn't want to leave them. I just wanted things to end the way they were. I know I can't come back now. I know I just can't take my life back. It was my choice to finish it, and I did it in a rage. I couldn't stop myself. I felt overwhelmed by what I was feeling. I couldn't see anything else. I was blinded ...'

As Mia spoke, I suddenly saw paramedics treating her at the scene, and knew Mia was referring to the moment after she had ended her life. Sharing this with Mia's father, I wrote: 'She's bringing me back to the paramedics who were treating her. She is saying that it didn't matter by then, that the die was cast. She is saying that life is like a game. You throw the dice and make the choice to take the actions that will create your pathway forward. She's telling me that there were others with her in spirit at that point. But they knew you and other family members needed some time to unfold through those final days when she was in hospital, and the decision to turn off life support with the learning it also brought. Those in spirit also knew she needed to wait and really see and experience how much it all affected you, and how much you actually did want her to survive.

'As Mia looked on, when her body was in the hospital being supported to breathe on the ventilator, it quickly became obvious to her that she was very much loved and cared for. She said you would often go out of the room and talk to her, and you knew she could hear you, as you sensed already that she was not there in her body. She said you were right, that she was actually there with you and listening to you. She is smiling at that ...

'She's moving my hands to the prayer position, showing me you were praying—that you prayed during that time. She wants you to know that you had angels around you then. She is saying that there were others from your family in spirit around you, and angels there too and personal guides of yours. She wants you to know they were there and they are actually still there with you.'

At that moment, Mia began to speak again in sentences rather than visions. 'So now, through my choice, I am here in spirit and you are there, and we can connect through Jess' mum, 'cause she can see me and talk to me, even though you can't. It's really helping me. I know you are all in pain, and I know you probably hate what I did, and I know you are all just trying to understand why I did it.

'I couldn't control it. I just did it. That was all. I didn't know it was going to end my life. I just knew it was going to end what was happening to me ... and what I did has caused you so much pain ... and I want to thank you for trying so hard to make things better for me. I can't come back now. I can't even speak to you or walk with you or be with you like before.

'I'm here because Jess' mum has made it easier for me to be here in this place. I want everyone to know that this place I am in now is really special, and really normal, and there are lots of people here, and they take care of me. There are other kids here who have chosen to end their life, and we come here and talk and understand what we did, and the consequences of the actions we took.

'We are not punished at all. It's not like that here. It's special. But we have to take time to think and learn and understand. Jess' mum would call it 'gaining wisdom' I guess. She kind of knows all this stuff, but I am going to tell you anyway ... she's like a halfway place, half there and half here. She sees us and works with us, and sees and works with people there where you are ... she does both. It's really cool.' With that, the message ended and Mia was gone.

In the late afternoon we loaded the car with Jessica's luggage. With heavy heart, I drove her to the airport. All the way down the expressway, I just wanted to reach out and hold her and not let her go. Watching her leave, I felt such emptiness inside. I just had to trust that she would be all right, and able to cope with the seventeen-hour journey back alone.

The days following Jessica's departure seemed like a blur. Before long, Mia visited again. I was sitting with the balcony door slightly open to the sunny afternoon, when she appeared through the doorway with a gentle, older woman. She was the sort of lady anyone adjusting to a new situation would cherish as a special mentor.

Ignoring me, they walked straight past. Mia was chatting to the woman. From what I could make out, she was explaining that this was the home where her friend, Jessica, lived. They disappeared around the corner walking towards the stairs. In my psychic vision, I could see them descending the stairs to Jessica's room. A short time later they reappeared where I sat at my desk. It was then I recognised that the older woman was the same lady who had appeared at the end of my bed several nights before.

As Mia began to speak, she was brimming with eagerness and enthusiasm. She talked of the book I'd write, explaining that she had been told that her story would be a part of my book. Being made aware of the impact it would have on others had offered her deeper meaning and higher purpose; it was as transformative for her as it had been for Shylo. Then moving past me back towards the doorway, the older lady who accompanied Mia placed a book into my hands—astonishingly, my book that would be published in the future! Momentarily glimpsing the spine of the book, I noticed the logo of Hay House Publishing. Mia and her special mentor had brought the book through time into my hands, so that I could feel the reality of it now. I sat staring at it in a state of wonderment. I could feel the book's significance and worth, and was aware of the encouragement I was being given from beyond the veil.

After what seemed like a long two weeks, Jessica returned from Mia's funeral. As she walked through the arrival gate, I wrapped my arms around her, embracing her with an enormous feeling of relief in my heart that she was home. At the same time I knew that after Mia's death, Jessica's life would never be the same. All I could do now was love and support her, give her what insight I could, but I couldn't take away her pain. I had to trust that Jessica would gain higher wisdom and understanding from this deeply painful experience.

The following day we drove to the nearby town of Medford, to take time out and go shopping. As we neared the shopping centre, Mia suddenly appeared in the back seat of the car. Hesitantly, I shared her appearance with Jessica. At that moment, Jessica and I both decided to shop at a particular store we had never shopped in before.

After several minutes of browsing, Jessica called out to me: 'Mum! Look!' She was clutching a bright yellow sign against her chest, as tears streamed down her face. 'Look! It's Mia's moose crossing sign! After all this time! I've been looking for two years, and I've finally found it! That last day at school before we left Australia, Mia was sad so I said I would buy her a present and send it to her. I asked her what she wanted, and she said a moose crossing sign. But I could never find one, until now.'

Wrapping Jessica up in my arms as she sobbed from the depths of her heart, I knew without doubt that Mia had guided us into the store. Jessica had done what was asked of her. She had found the sign Mia wanted. And in finding the sign, Mia had been given a sign of the continuance of the life of her dear friend, and of the love and friendship they would continue to share. In her own way, Mia was letting Jessica know that Jessica had done all she could, and that there was nothing more Jessica could have done to prevent what had happened.

It was time now for Jessica to forgive; to forgive herself. 'Mum, it's her moose crossing sign!' she repeated with such palpable relief. 'This is what she wanted! I found it. I found the sign she wanted after all!'

ONE TINY GRAIN
OF SAND

An early spring heralded the completion of another school year, and the coming of spring break. I knew I had to make some significant decisions about our future. During spring break, we flew to Los Angeles as I had clients to see there and friends to visit. It also gave Jessica the opportunity to shop for a dress to wear to the senior prom she had been invited to.

We took a moment in our busy schedule to enjoy some relaxing morning tea in a café, amid the usual open laptops, people chasing deadlines, old friends enjoying leisurely gossip, and informal business meetings over coffee. Finding an empty table, Jessica and I chatted while she synchronised my laptop with Starbucks' wireless internet connection.

Casually surveying the café, I noticed behind me a budding starlet was nervously pitching her talent to a laid-back agent. He had likely heard it all before—and likely she had too. In her constant questioning, I could hear those universal questions: *Am I enough? Am I what he is looking for? Does he see my potential?* This limiting outlook was clearly dictating the outcome of the meeting, as it does for all of us. How challenging life is when we're stuck repeating our same limiting small story. And how different life can be once we heal and move beyond it and embody our true potential!

To my left was a thin, middle-aged man wearing an old, white singlet. He sat fidgeting with a lime-green telephone receiver from the seventies, strapped with duct tape to an out-of-date towelling headband. The contrasts in Beverly Hills were always fascinating.

Finishing my peppermint hot chocolate, I playfully announced: 'I've tried coffee cup readings before but never hot chocolate. Today, it's going to be a hot chocolate reading!' I said this for a bit of light comic relief. Yet the crossroads I was at and the decisions I faced were intense. Jessica needed stability, consistency. She needed home. I was determined to create that for her, and to make the world a better place. I also felt a yearning to return home.

For almost all my life North America felt like that place for me. Yet I knew now I had to go deeper. I had to find that place of home within. The most difficult part was to let go of what I wanted, and move to where the universe seemed to be guiding me.

I didn't regret coming to the US. How could I when I'd been privileged to witness such an incredible sequence of events? My experiences were traumatic and transformative. They had woven a profound spiritual tapestry for me that warmed my heart and liberated my soul. I longed to share these transformative possibilities with others.

Now I knew without any doubt that life was eternal, that our physical life here on the earth plane was for our soul's growth, and that when we reach the end of our earthly life, we move into a light-filled place of luminous consciousness. And it is there where we continue our soul's expression, until we are ready to return to physical form and grow even more. This place in spirit is a place of non-judgement and unconditional regard, of compassion and truth that transcends all sense of separation and difference.

So, right now as I sat with my hot chocolate in Los Angeles, I had to trust in the greater plan to guide me home. In this lighthearted moment with Jessica in Starbucks, my mind drifted to the bottom of my now empty hot chocolate. Peering into the cup, I turned it slightly to the left, then slightly to the right. Entering the 'zone,' the energy effortlessly changed.

One moment, I was simply observing the vision shown to me. The next I was entering that vision. I was standing on Balmoral Beach in Sydney. Memories of countless happy days at the beach with the family flooded my mind, with my dad hiding away in his eagle's nest out of the sun enjoying a good book, while my mother with her olive skin, dark hair and fabulous figure sunbaked in her bikini. It was all so vivid! I stood quietly by the water's edge, taking in hundreds of tiny beach memories of the past, contemplating the endings and new beginnings my life's journey had brought me thus far. Then crouching down, I picked up some sand in my right hand, and let it slip slowly through my fingers.

Suddenly, I was no longer alone. John, Mia and Shylo were standing around me. I was so moved by their unexpected visitation at this big time for me, moved by their dedication, their fearlessness, their love and concern for humanity.

Looking down to my hand once more, I noticed the many tiny grains of sand and how quickly they fell through my fingers and dropped into the ocean of sand below. Capturing one of the remaining grains of sand, I wondered whether ... **in all the oceans of sand, one tiny grain of sand could truly make a difference?**

John's voice pierced through my moment of reflection: 'We are a tiny spark within an infinite cosmos, attempting to play out a role filled with complexities, looking for some higher spiritual and more profound meaning to our existence. What is pivotal is to create the necessary elements needed to change how we feel, to change what we believe ourselves to be. This means digging deeper within ourselves, unmasking and untangling the disorder created from our past, transmuting the pain and dislodging our limited thinking, moving it to new levels of awareness. This is why we come here to earth. Not for our self-satisfaction, but for our spiritual evaluation. It's a metamorphosis of the spirit.

'We can all make a difference, if we are willing to recognise the parts of ourselves that lie dormant within each of us, the aspects that are devalued, misunderstood. We can turn the tide once we realise how different our lives can be, when we honour the true nature and broader reality of non-ordinary experiences, accepting these as normal, and free ourselves from the confines our limited worldview has placed upon us in ignorant action.'

My heart was radiant with love for each of these beautiful souls. I continued to listen, as Shylo then began to talk to me and to all those who want to bring about a shift in their lives: 'The world needs us to know that we are so close to extinction, that the trees and animals are doomed if we don't listen. All we ask is you open your hearts and minds to the wondrous life beyond what you know, beyond what you've been taught. There is so much more than I ever knew, and it took me to end my life before I saw that just one voice, just one grain of sand, can truly make a difference.

'The only thing that stops that one voice is the failure of that one voice to realise its true potential. We are not limited beings. We are capable of profound possibilities. We are capable of creating a life for all that only some on earth have begun to dream of.'

There was a sudden pause. Glancing from Shylo to John then across to Mia, the enormous love I felt for each of them pulsated through me, reached out across time and space. There was such a connection, a oneness of voice and vision. I felt a gathering of force and spirit, ready to reach out to the heart of our humanity, desperately needing to awaken us.

And it was then that their united voice spoke out: 'We must move from the head and begin to seat ourselves in our heart, to own our true power, to unite as one interconnected force of light across the planet. We have come here to unite your hearts, to move into action and create a song that will play out and be recognised in every country, every city. We, the voices beyond the veil, send you those privileged to visit the earth with a message of truth and hope. We stand united, bathed in the light and wonder that life can be for all. Our only hope is that you will listen.'

ABOUT THE AUTHOR

For over twenty-five years, Elizabeth Robinson has assisted people throughout the world to gain insight, clarity and empowerment. She is an experienced professional counsellor and coach who is highly regarded internationally as a powerful intuitive and visionary. Born and raised in Australia, she was educated at the University of NSW in Sydney.

With great expertise, Elizabeth makes the invisible, visible. Her private consultations and public events skillfully combine the metaphysical and the psychological. Her signature en-masse energy transmissions to entire audiences, working one-on-one and with the entire crowd, offer remarkable transformative experiences like no other. Using her extraordinary multisensory and multidimensional abilities to access the unseen and unspoken, Elizabeth offers powerful insight, inspiration and transformation.

Elizabeth's passion is to awaken and inspire others to know and live their true potential. Website: www.wingsofwisdom.com.au

We hope you enjoyed this Hay House book. If you'd like to receive our online catalogue featuring additional information on Hay House books and products, or if you'd like to find out more about the Hay Foundation, please contact:

Hay House, Inc.,
P.O. Box 5100, Carlsbad, CA 92018-5100
Phone: (760) 431-7695 • *Fax:* (760) 431-6948
www.hayhouse.com® • www.hayfoundation.org

***

Published and distributed in Australia by:
Hay House Australia Pty. Ltd.,
18/36 Ralph St., Alexandria NSW 2015
Phone: +61 2 9669 4299 • *Fax:* +61 2 9669 4144
www.hayhouse.com.au

Published and distributed in the United Kingdom by:
Hay House UK, Ltd., Astley House, 33 Notting Hill Gate,
London, W11 3JQ • *Phone:* 44-203-675-2450
Fax: 44-203-675-2451 • www.hayhouse.co.uk

Published and distributed in the Republic of South Africa by:
Hay House SA (Pty), Ltd., P.O. Box 990, Witkoppen 2068
info@hayhouse.co.za • www.hayhouse.co.za

Published in India by: Hay House Publishers India, Muskaan Complex,
Plot No. 3, B-2, Vasant Kunj, New Delhi 110 070
Phone: 91-11-4176-1620 • *Fax:* 91-11-4176-1630
www.hayhouse.co.in

Distributed in Canada by:
Raincoast Books, 2440 Viking Way, Richmond, B.C. V6V 1N2
Phone: 1-800-663-5714 • *Fax:* 1-800-565-3770 • www.raincoast.com

***

<u>Access New Knowledge.</u>
<u>Anytime. Anywhere.</u>

Learn and evolve at your own pace with the world's leading experts.

www.hayhouseU.com